Democratic Parenting's

3 Reasons
for Behavior

Why kids act out.   The checklist.

REASON 1

Needs:
Does your child have a legitimate unmet need?

Is your child's behavior in response to a legitimate unmet need? There are 14 important needs to consider. These are the needs for healthy nutrition, exercise, security, healing, routine, nurturing environment, social belonging, participation, appropriate stimulation, affection, attention, autonomy, information or creative expression.

REASON 2

Stress:
Is your child emotional, tense, confused, stressed?

Is your child upset, emotional, tense, worried, confused or stressed about something? There are four types of stress for kids: Active stress, passive stress, situational stress or birth stress. Symptoms of emotional stress are: whining, demanding, tension or desperation in their voice. Seeming distracted, distant, avoiding eye contact, gets upset easily, tantrums, crying, raging or aggressive outbursts and backtalk. Democratic Parenting shows you what to do when your child gets stressed.

REASON 3

Role Models:
What examples are your children modeling?

These are all the people in your child's life. The more time your child spends with them, the more characteristics they will model. Role models provide the example of how to relate and communicate with the world. Parents are the primary role models usually. Then family, friends, babysitters, teachers and everyone else that your child is exposed to. Children are natural mimics. Even models of behavior from the fictional characters in our story books, TV channels, and movies can cause our kids to do and say inappropriate things.

www.Democratic-Parenting.com

From the Desk of Blaise T. Ryan

Dear Parent,

Thank you for buying our book. We hope you like it. If you do, give out some of these bookmarks to your friends and your family. You can also come share your stories with us on facebook.com/raisinghappykids.

Don't forget to claim your six free bonuses that come with this book at *www.ParentLearningClub.com*.

On the other side, you'll find The 3 Reasons for Behavior Checklist. Hang it on your fridge. It is a helpful reminder.

Sincerely,
Blaise

*"We never know the love of a parent
till we become parents ourselves."*
~ *Henry Ward Beecher*

Share your stories with us on Facebook.

Phone us: 1-877-311-2724
Email us: support@parentlearningclub.com
Facebook us: facebook.com/raisinghappykids
Visit us: www.ParentLearningClub.com

ParentLearningClub™
Raising Happy Kids, Together!

Democratic Parenting

Blaise T. Ryan

CONTENTS

"Your children are not your children.
They are the sons and daughters of Life's longing for itself.
They come through you but not from you,
And though they are with you yet they belong not to you.

You may give them your love but not your thoughts,
For they have their own thoughts.
You may house their bodies but not their souls,
For their souls dwell in the house of tomorrow,
which you cannot visit, not even in your dreams.
You may strive to be like them,
but seek not to make them like you.
For life goes not backward nor tarries with yesterday.

You are the bows from which your children
as living arrows are sent forth.
The archer sees the mark upon the path of the infinite,
and He bends you with His might
that His arrows may go swift and far.
Let your bending in the archer's hand be for gladness;
For even as He loves the arrow that flies,
so He loves also the bow that is stable."

- Khalil Gibran

HOW TO USE THIS GUIDEBOOK

*F*irst, if you ordered the downloadable e-book, we recommend that you print it out for easy reference. You can either staple it together or punch holes in it and put it in a binder. You may also want to order a printed version too, which you can do on our website at *www.parentlearningclub.com.*

Print out the reference sheet: "3 Reasons for Misbehavior" in Chapter 3. Then put it on your refrigerator—you'll find it very helpful to have these reminders in front of you during the day.

Stay connected! Make sure you visit our Facebook page to stay connected with the authors of this e-book and other parents who are actively raising happy and cooperative kids. Search "Raising Happy Kids" on Facebook, or go to facebook.com/ RaisingHappyKids and click the "Like" button. This is a great place to get extra tips, ask questions about the program, and learn from other parents.

Access the free bonus resource area online. Download additional material, recordings, reports, and workbooks by logging in to your ParentLearningClub.com member account. An appendix at the end of this book describes each one of the bonuses.

Read our emails. We send you a lot of supportive guidance, tips, important medical research and study results, as well as interesting, real-life stories from other parents. If you haven't yet received any emails from us, make sure to add our email address to your email address book: support@parentlearningclub.com.

Sometimes, your settings may send our emails to your junk or spam folders, so check there for any missed messages. Make sure to add the above address to your own address book so that you don't miss any important information we send you.

On our website, you can sign up for courses, counseling, coaching, or you can learn more about working with us. Just go to www.ParentLearningClub.com.

RAISING A CHILD IS NOT EASY

> *"We never know the love of a parent till we become parents ourselves."*
>
> *- Henry Ward Beecher*

The terrible twos, trying threes, fearsome fours, furious fives, scary sixes, all the way to the rebellious teens! With so many "difficult" ages and stages, are there any years when parents get to enjoy their kids?

We believe these are overused stereotypes. **We believe every day with your child can and should be a magical one. Every week should be memorable. Every year should be a treasure.**

But we also know that sometimes the demands of our busy lives get in the way: our careers, work, bills, obligations, and other duties fight for our daily attention. All this stress affects us—and it affects our children!

Yes, raising a child is not easy—**it takes effort, patience, and inner strength.** Occasional clashes between parent and child happen to all of us, but, when challenging behaviors such as defiance, tantrums, backtalk and even hitting become a daily occurrence, it can drive even the most patient parents over the edge.

The skills taught in *Democratic Parenting* have been described as a powerful "cooperation button." All you have to do is read it and apply its lessons, and you can press that button any time you need to. The book teaches a core set of parenting skills—real life, real world, practical skills. *Democratic Parenting* will teach you how to lead a harmonious life with your children.

Keep in mind that it's common for some parents when they first read this guide to feel a bit daunted by everything they have to do to uncover their own "cooperation button". But most parents quickly realize that they are already using some of the democratic methods described within. Most of the time you just need to adjust a few things, be more consistent in your approach, a little more careful in your communication, eliminate the use of punishment and rewards, and you're well on the way!

This guide will help to strengthen your parenting where it's too permissive and become more flexible where it's too authoritarian. Consider it yoga for your parenting.

As with yoga, we approach parenting and your family as a whole. All the 14 methods we describe in this guide work together in synergy to bring balance, peace and harmony into your family relationships. If you try to use one method independently, without putting the full system of democratic parenting into practice, you will likely find the results less then ideal. So enjoy this book as many times as you need to. Many parents tell us they read it repeatedly, using it as a reference when issues come up.

The real key to making this system work for you is getting enough "me time." You need to keep your own emotional gas tank filled up. Otherwise, how can you have patience when your child pushes your buttons at the most inconvenient times? In order to listen to your child, you need to have someone listen to you. To keep your emotional fuel tank topped up, schedule your life so you get enough time every day, or every week, to rejuvenate and replenish yourself.

We believe that life is fundamentally good and that our children are the manifestation of that goodness. **If you share this belief, this book is for you.** Take the time to enjoy this good life, with your family, and without them. It is a balance that takes time, practice and devotion to find. This book will help give you some practical methods to achieve this balance – and it is up to you to put it all together.

Children make us hyper-sensitive to the speed at which time flies. It's a race just to keep up with them! And, like all parents, you probably want nothing more than to just enjoy as many special moments with your child as possible.

These moments are their gift to us—to remind us of the meaning of life—but too often we miss them. We are so distracted by our day-to-day chores and responsibilities that we miss out on the special and profound moments our children's innocence give us.

Behavior is not a "stage in life," it's a response. We all understand this intuitively, but we can easily forget it. There is always a REASON for behavior issues, but much of the time what triggers the behavior is not the true cause of it. The cause is usually a deeper, unmet need, a stress, an environmental or physiological issue that is causing the behavior response.

11

Children think and feel differently than adults. The way we see the world and the way they do are rarely the same. By understanding how the developing child's mind works, we can literally access the child's "cooperation button."

By using simple techniques, all described in detail in the following chapters, you will learn **a whole new way of connecting with your child.** You will develop a bond with your child that is so deep and loving, it will transform your life.

What you will learn from this program:

- The difference between authoritarian, permissive, and democratic discipline. Which is the best method? When should you use each one? And why?

- The effects of bribes and rewards, and how these short-term solutions can result in worse behavior later on—and what to do instead.

- What causes children to become frustrated, distracted and over-stimulated—and most importantly, how to help your child express frustration in a healthy and safe way.

- Fun games that melt frustrations, sibling rivalry, and resistance, and how to play them with one child or many.

- How methods such as *Self-Directed Play* and *Play Attention Time* can transform even the most defiant, distracted, and upset child into the sweet child you know is hiding inside.

- Five magic words and phrases used in our *Connective Communication* method to help your child listen, pay attention, and behave.

- How to *Set Limits* that children respect and follow, without raising your voice or using punishments.

- What to do and what not to do during *Family Meetings*, with important pointers—from beginning the meeting to closing the meeting—on how to make this time so special your kids will look forward to it.

- Guidelines for how to use *Natural Consequences*, which foster clear thinking and good judgment in your child. You'll no longer need to use harsh discipline methods.

- How to peer-pressure-proof your children, improve their communication, and give them the best opportunities for social success in life through specific ways of relating and listening to them.

- What you need to know about television, video games, sugar, sleep and exercise. The balance is easier to reach than you may think.

Are you ready to start down a new path on your journey as a parent? It's time to get started with *Democratic Parenting*.

"If I had my child to raise over again:
I'd build self-esteem first and the house later.
I'd finger paint more and point the finger less.
I would do less correcting and more connecting.
I'd take my eyes off my watch and watch with my eyes.
I would care to know less and know to care more.
I'd take more hikes and fly more kites.
I'd stop playing serious and seriously play...
I would run through more fields and gaze at more stars.
I'd do more hugging and less tugging.
I'd see the oak tree in the acorn more often.
I would be firm less often and affirm much more.
I'd model less about the love of power.
And more about the power of love."

- Diane Loomans

DID YOU FORGET YOUR BONUSES?

Before you start your journey, we promised you some bonuses. So allow us to explain what they are and how you can access them. If you bought your book from Amazon or another retailer, then you are eligible to access these free bonuses online - immediately!

If you bought the book, you are already half way there and it means you care about your child's future and your family's happiness. To make sure that the efforts you put towards building a strong and beautiful relationship with your children really work, we are offering you **six free bonuses**. These bonuses complement the book, significantly helping you achieve your goals by reinforcing the lessons in this guide.

The bonuses are a comprehensive set of e-mail based e-courses, audio mp3 exclusive interviews and reports. Get true, practical advice from world-famous parenting experts and doctors such as Naomi Aldort, PhD; Dr. Haiman; Dr. Robert Brooks and more.

Learn about:

- 7 Effective Alternatives to Punishment
- Dietary Tips to Help with Child Misbehavior, ADD/ADHD, Obesity and Poor Health
- Teaching Children Respect
- Post-Natal Depression
- 5 Reasons to Stop Saying "Good Job"
- Teaching Through Love Instead of Fear
- How to Raise a Happy and Cooperative Child with

Half the Effort

• What Every Parent Needs to Know about Discipline, Punishment and Rules

• How to Raise a Resilient Child

Make sure you become a parenting expert too by signing up to get the bonuses, sent directly to your inbox! All for free!

All you have to do is forward the Amazon receipt, or if you bought it in a store, take a picture or scan your receipt (your "proof of purchase") to the following e-mail address and we will get them right to you!

Forward your receipt to:
SUPPORT@PARENTLEARNINGCLUB.COM

These bonuses are amazing; you do not want to miss out. One mother told us that as she was listening to one of the bonus interviews, a switch flipped inside her and she just "got it." Within a week her relationship with her daughter blossomed! Motherhood became what she had always dreamed it would be!

We want you to share in that same experience. There may be a golden nugget of insight or information that could transform your life. Forward your Amazon or other retail receipt to *support@ParentLearningClub.com* and we'll get you access ASAP.

Sincerely,
Blaise

CHAPTER 1

FOCUS ON THE ROOT, NOT THE FRUIT

> *"No one knows how children will turn out; a great tree often springs from a tender plant."*
>
> *– Norwegian proverb*

*I*magine you had an apple tree, and, as the apples grew on the tree, instead of being red and healthy, they were yellow, brown, deformed, and rotten. Now imagine that you asked someone what to do, and he gave you this advice: *"First...,"* he said, *"Get some red paint and color each one. Then, if that doesn't work, go to the market and buy a bushel of apples and replace the rotten ones with the fresh, healthy ones."*

This advice sounds foolish because it doesn't actually fix the problem; it just hides it. This temporary fix will make the tree appear, to the undiscerning eye, as if it's producing healthy apples. Unfortunately, for as long as the tree's roots go ignored, its fruit continues to rot.

17

This is the same approach many parents and disciplinarians use when confronted by a child's challenging behavior. The behavior itself—be it defiance, temper tantrums, hyperactivity, timidity, violence, poor focus, or any behavior we see—all represent the "fruit." The reason for the child's behavior—his underlying needs and emotional state—represents the "root."

Using punishments, rewards, bribes, threats, negotiations, distractions, promises, or even medication in order to "discipline" your child's behavior are all akin to painting the apples red—because the emphasis is on the behavior, not the cause. This is why these methods of discipline are short-lived in their effectiveness. The difficult behaviors, like the rotten apples, resurface in time because their underlying reasons have yet to be addressed.

Children do not misbehave without reason....Children learn everything in life the same way they learn how to walk and talk—by modeling the examples around them.

In fact, regardless of what you do, your child will undoubtedly follow your example—for better or worse—just as they follow the examples all around them. They model behaviors they see on TV, in kids at school, in characters in storybooks, and from observing the adults around them.

Children inherit both the best and worst attributes of their parents. This is why parenting is truly the original self-development program. You can't ask for a better "life coach" or "guru" because no one else will hold you more accountable to your own integrity than your child. If you want your child to listen, you should listen to her. If you want her to pay attention to you, you need to pay attention to her—without distractions, without multi-tasking. No matter what you tell your children, no matter how many lectures you give them, they will model your actions more than follow your words.

While most discipline methods that address the behavior work at first, they quickly lose their power, just as the rotting eventually shows through the painted apples.

Parents who uses punishments long enough will soon discover that the child soon becomes immune to the punishment as their resentment builds and defiance becomes more and more overt.

The same applies to using rewards. The child will eventually demand increasingly appealing rewards to keep him on side because the true problem with rewards is that they are nothing more than a bribe. These bribes may eventually corrupt a child's desire to cooperate, participate and help out.

Democratic Parenting and the methodology within this book focus on effective ways to respond to the underlying reasons for the challenging behavior. Often, the parents can ignore the behavior itself while they address the root issue directly. In order to do this effectively, the underlying reason needs to be understood, found, and addressed.

Using the example of the apple tree, we can see that the first step to healing the tree is figuring out why it's producing rotten fruit. Is it an infestation of bugs? Is there a disease? Do the roots need more water? Is the soil missing nutrients? Once the real needs of the tree are ascertained, then our response focuses on providing those needs.

"The trick to problem solving is to go to the root, i.e. to find the actual cause. When we find and work at removing the actual cause of the problem we will never find it repeating."

- Brahma Kumaris

CHAPTER 2

3 KINDS OF PARENTING AND DISCIPLINE

> *"Children Learn What They Live.*
> *If a child lives with hostility, he learns to fight.*
> *If a child lives with ridicule, he learns to be shy.*
> *If a child learns to feel shame, he learns to feel guilty.*
> *If a child lives with tolerance, he learns to be patient.*
> *If a child lives with encouragement, he learns confidence.*
> *If a child lives with security, he learns to have faith.*
> *If a child lives with approval, he learns to like himself.*
> *If a child lives with acceptance and friendship, he learns to find love in the world."*
>
> *- Dorothy Law Nolte*

Over the last century, there have been many break-throughs in understanding child developmental psychology and parenting education. Authoritarian or punitive discipline has been practiced since humanity began, and, until very recently, was regarded as the only way to discipline a child. The biggest weakness in this approach is that the discipline is dependent on an external, authoritarian control. However, with the global shift towards democracy, this kind of control is less effective than ever as it doesn't promote cooperation[1].

As the world's socio-political landscape shifts from dictatorship to democracy, so too have parenting methods begun to shift. Teachers no longer have the right to physically hit their students as they did up until the recent past. In the modern, democratic world, children have the same rights as their parents; they are no longer viewed as their parents' property.

Through this global movement, recent generations have seen parents purposefully reject authoritarian models and adopt what we call permissive parenting. The problem with permissive parenting is that kids are often granted too much freedom without enough positive direction and limits. This usually results in out-of-control behaviors. Eventually even permissive parents lose their patience and, like pendulums, swing over to an authoritarian model of discipline in order to establish some order and control.

We can therefore see that on one extreme we have authoritarian parenting, and, on the other, we have permissive parenting. This book proposes a third model, which we will call democratic parenting.

All parents are role models for their kids. Authoritarian parents model dominance of power, so their kids test their power through defiance and rebellion. Permissive parents use bribes, threats, and negotiations to get their kids to cooperate, so the children learn how to negotiate and manipulate. Democratic parents treat their kids with respect, thus their kids return this trust by cooperating easily. Let's look at these three models more closely.

1 Dreikus, R., 1991.

AUTHORITARIAN PARENTING

> *"We live in a sort of fear that our children will grow up badly, learn bad habits, develop wrong attitudes, do things the wrong way. We watch over them constantly and try to prevent some mistake. We are constantly correcting and admonishing. Such an approach shows lack of faith in our children; it is humiliating and discouraging...With all the emphasis on the negative, where can we expect the child to find the energy to proceed towards achievement?"*
>
> *- Rudolf Dreikurs*

A study on how authoritarian parenting affects social competence came to this conclusion: *"Children from authoritarian parenting lack social competence as the parent generally predicts what the child should do instead of allowing the child to choose by him or herself. The children also rarely take initiative. They are socially withdrawn and look to others to decide what's right. These children lack spontaneity and lack curiosity."* [2]

Another long-term study of children who were raised with authoritarian discipline found, *"These children are often the most vulnerable to enter into relationships with, or marry equally abusive and controlling partners, or develop mental illness when they enter adulthood."* [3]

[2] (Baumrind, The Influence of parenting style on adolescent competence ans substance use, 1991) (Miller, Cowan, Cowen, & Hetherington, 1993) (Weiss & Schwarz, 1996)
[3] (Baumrind, Rearing competent children, 1978)

23

Parents who use authoritarian discipline will tend to either use violent or non-violent means to enforce their rule. First, let's look at authoritarian violent discipline.

AUTHORITARIAN VIOLENT

With this kind of discipline, the parent maintains all the control in the relationship through physical or psychological intimidation, violence, or abuse. Methods such as hitting, spanking, threatening, yelling, cursing, scolding, belittling, humiliation, blaming, criticizing, harsh punishments, and similar tactics are used.

This sounds awful when listed like this, does it not? But most parents don't even realize they are doing this. The home atmosphere will be tense, rigid, oppressive, and domineering. With this form of parenting, children will often feel angry, resentful, hostile, scared, and powerless. This approach fosters low self-esteem.

What children learn from authoritarian violent discipline:

- To act out and use violence and aggression to deal with situations is an accepted method
- To be hurtful towards others—siblings, peers, family, or friends—in order to obtain what they want
- To obey blindly out of fear
- To compete against siblings and parents
- To lie and escape responsibility
- To feel powerless, incompetent, and bad
- To resent and rebel against authority

- To have hostility and anger towards the world
- To have low self-esteem
- To suppress their pain, which can lead to drug abuse and coping habits
- Lack of self-discipline

Teens raised in authoritarian violent homes will tend to rebel strongly and aggressively. They may run away from home, act out, get into fights, hang out with the wrong crowd, get into drugs, engage in sexual promiscuity, and get into other trouble. This is all in an attempt to have their unmet needs for social belonging, affection, security, autonomy, and attention satisfied.

As you can see, the authoritarian parent ultimately runs out of power, just as violent political dictators are eventually overthrown by an angry population who are hungry for equality and autonomy.

Why You Should Never Spank or Hit Your Child

A Canadian government study[4] for children at risk showed that being hit as a child was directly associated with depressive symptoms and psychiatric disorders as adults. Furthermore, a landmark meta-analysis of eighty-eight corporal punishment research studies spanning over six decades showed that corporal punishment of children was associated with negative outcomes including increased delinquent and antisocial behavior and increased risk of child abuse and spousal abuse.

Studies have shown that the more parents spanked children for antisocial behavior, the more the antisocial behavior

---

4 (McMillian, Boyle, Wong, Duku, Fleming, & Walsh, 1999)

increased. When children are hit, they learn that violence is an acceptable means to express frustration or to get what they want. Consequently, children who are physically punished will often tend to hit other children.

AUTHORITARIAN NON-VIOLENT PARENTING

Material and emotional control are the distinguishing characteristics of this style of parenting. Passive-aggressive manipulation is used without the overt violence demonstrated by authoritarian violent discipline. Rewards and punishments are the primary methods used to keep control.

Material control is maintained through bribes such as money, treats, and toys; and through privileges such as video game and TV time, movies, outings, or other activities or freedoms. Parents can be overheard saying things such as, "If you're a good boy today, you will get that toy you want." Consequently, the punitive side of this control is that the reward is not deserved.

Emotional control is also maintained by demonstrating affections of praise, love, attention, or even hugs and snuggling as rewards. In democratic parenting, these affections are given unconditionally regardless of the child's performance or behavior. The difference is marked when authoritarian non-violent parents withhold these affections as a form of punishment. Other common methods of discipline include isolation, criticism, guilt, and punitive consequences. Time-outs, low scores on reward charts, grounding, being sent out of the class, fewer rewards, and lectures are forms of punishment used.

What children learn from authoritarian non-violent discipline:

- Conformity
- Deviousness
- To lie in order to avoid the punishment or get the reward
- Fierce competitiveness and rivalries often come out between siblings or classmates
- Lack self-discipline
- To desire increasingly large rewards
- To be motivated by promises or fears
- To pay attention and cooperate only when it serves them

Children raised with authoritarian non-violent parenting may feel resentful, angry, misunderstood, and manipulated. As their needs go unmet, they find themselves in a continual state of anxiety from wanting the reward and fearing the punishment.

The adolescent teen will withdraw emotionally, rebel, and search elsewhere for attention or affection. Parents who practice this form of discipline most commonly complain that their teenager doesn't talk with them or that they don't know how to "get through" to their seemingly troubled teen.

Because the parent dominates the power in the relationship, the child's need for autonomy goes unmet. Because autonomy is one of their primary needs, whenever children suppress it, they will automatically exert their autonomy through defiance, rebellion, and power struggles. As long as their need for autonomy is not satisfied, they will reject participation and cooperation within the family.

The only recourse to the authoritarian parent caught in this kind of power struggle with a child or teen is to double up their efforts at control. This usually takes the form of increasing the pleasure of gaining the promised rewards or increasing the pain of the punishments.

Both options only widen the gap of disconnection between parent and child as the battle for power becomes fiercer the longer the reasons for the behaviors go unaddressed.

Authoritarian parents need to learn to be less firm and more flexible.

PERMISSIVE PARENTING

"Where parents do too much for their children, the children will not do much for themselves."

- Elbert Hubbard

*P*ermissive parenting is the polar opposite of authoritarian parenting. While authoritarian parents dominate and control, permissive parents have no control. In this style, rules are not enforced and there is little or no respect for order or limits. Thus, chaos reigns supreme in the permissive parent's home. In order to establish some kind of order, the permissive parent will, out of frustration and exasperation, end up using authoritarian methods.

Permissive parents tend to use pleading, negotiating, nagging, yielding, lecturing, talking, bribes, rewards, waiting, self-sacrificing, rescuing, and catering to their child's whims in order to achieve some cooperation. Just as in authoritarian discipline, the focus remains on the superficial behaviors of the child, while the underlying reasons remain unaddressed. As a result, the cooperation and harmony achieved with the child is short-lived, and his or her behavior continues to deteriorate over time.

With permissive parenting, the home atmosphere can be chaotic, messy, unordered, and inconsistent. Parents often feel exhausted, unappreciated, helpless, disrespected, and resentful. The parent will often be very concerned about their child's behaviors and may consequently feel as if they need to "rescue" or make special allowances for their child. This can develop in many ways. Some parents may tend towards spoiling their children, while others will smother them, continually trying to correct them or cater to their desires and whims.

It's quite common for one parent to tend towards authoritarian discipline, while the other tends to be more permissive. It's kind of like the good cop, bad cop approach; however, the difference is not a premeditated strategy to manipulate their kids. It more often tends to be a source of discontent between parents. Usually the father will tend to be more authoritarian while the mother is more permissive. However, it can also happen in reverse, just as sometimes both parents will use one model or the other.

Parents who tend towards authoritarian discipline will often criticize permissive parents as being too lenient and easy on their kids. Permissive parents will say that authoritarian parents are too harsh and critical with their kids.

While permissive parents also use rewards and punishments, the difference is that permissive parents use them as a last resort when they are tired of being ignored and overrun by their out-of-control kids. When permissive parents lose their patience, they may slip into violent or non-violent authoritarianism, depending entirely on the personal characteristics and upbringing of the parent.

Permissive parents have a very hard time saying "no" and setting limits with their kids. Whenever they try to set a limit, the child will often ignore it with little or no consequence. Permissive parents tend to be too flexible and need to learn how to be more firm. Children raised in this type of discipline will have difficulty controlling themselves and will tend to act very impulsively.

Characteristics children learn/adopt from permissive parenting:

* To be selfish and inconsiderate

* To be demanding, whiny, needy, and overly dependent

* To dominate and control their parents

* To be manipulative and passive aggressive

* To be irresponsible, especially teens

* To be skilled at triggering the parent's emotional buttons

* To be insecure and confused by the parent's rotating moods

* To feel guilty and identify with their weaknesses and insufficiencies

* To be disrespectful of authority

* To be messy, disorganized, and disorderly

Teens raised with this type of discipline are usually allowed to do whatever they want. Often they are permitted to go anywhere with anyone until anytime. They will tend to be irresponsible with this freedom and dismissive of any potential consequences of their actions. This attitude usually gets them into trouble with authorities, which they are quick to try to ignore or brush-over.

Most commonly, parents will use a mixture of permissive and authoritarian methods. Often their approach is dependent on their mood. When they are in a good mood, they will be more permissive, and, when they are tense, tired, or in a bad mood, they will act more authoritarian. This is the main reason why children raised this way will often feel confused and insecure. They are forever unsure about what the real limits are because those limits are always dependent on the emotional state of their parents.

DEMOCRATIC PARENTING

"My father didn't tell me how to live; he lived, and let me watch him do it."

-Clarence Budinton Kelland

Democratic parenting's primary method of discipline is through establishing and maintaining a sense of connection with the child. Being connected to the child not only opens the doors to understanding the underlying reasons for their behaviors, but it also ensures that the child feels included in the process. When children feel included in the family, half of their defiance will disappear.

Because children are entirely dependent on their parents for their survival, their need to feel connected to their parents is one of their most important needs. For children to enjoy life and have good, age-appropriate judgment, this sense of connection to other people and to their environment needs to be strong and secure. They need to feel as if they belong and that they hold significant status within life.

In authoritarian parenting, the parent has all the power in the relationship. In permissive parenting, the parent has zero power. With democratic parenting, everyone has a sense of power—including the child. When the parents and children share the sense of power, there is no need for power struggles, which makes cooperation natural and easy.

The methods used for democratic parenting allow the home atmosphere to be relaxed, orderly, and flexible. The parents provide unconditional love, modeling, and encouragement, and they listen to feelings and have Natural Consequences for their children. Democratic parenting focuses on anticipating and meeting their child's underlying needs. The parents seek first to understand where their child is "at" emotionally, mentally, and developmentally before they respond to any behavior.

The home atmosphere is relaxed, flexible, and united. Regular family meetings are incorporated into the family routine and held in a supportive and encouraging atmosphere. These regular meetings provide a venue for children and parents to resolve issues together. This teaches children to focus on finding solutions that meet everyone's needs.

Because the atmosphere helps children feel connected and loved, and their thinking and ideas are incorporated in family decision-making, children feel happy, secure, and gain confidence in their abilities and judgment.

Children raised with democratic discipline tend to have high self-esteem because their needs for attention, affection, connection, autonomy, and participation are topped up. Consequently, they do not easily fall prey to peer pressure or external manipulation.

What children learn from democratic modeling:

- Self-discipline and self-control
- Responsibility for their actions
- Respect and consideration for family and their community
- Intelligent thinking and cooperation
- Good judgment and problem solving
- Non-violent communication skills
- Optimism and a good sense of humor
- Appreciation and gratitude
- To trust their parent's direction and guidance
- How to negotiate for the benefit of everyone

What we then see in the adolescent teen is love and respect between the parents and the child. Because they feel loved and connected to their parents, they feel no need to rebel, withdraw, or seek inappropriate attention elsewhere.

The methods of democratic parenting are presented in this book. The common theme for all these methods is continually brought back to two things: First, you need clarity regarding the underlying root cause of any challenging behavior. Is it due to unmet needs? Stress? Or another reason? Secondly, all the methods rely on maintaining or establishing a strong sense of connection with the child. What's important to keep in mind is that it's your child's sense of connection, not yours, which is vital. Even if you feel totally connected with your child, the success of these methods depends on *their* sense of connection with you.

When you approach any difficult behavior with these two things in mind, you will initiate a transformation in your child. Now it's time to jump into the democratic parenting methodology and how to get started with it.

> *"Parents can tell, but never teach, unless they practice what they preach."*
>
> *- Arnold Glasow*

Important points:

- Punishments and rewards may work in the short term but have negative consequences in the end.
- Authoritarian Parenting causes parents to run out of power because the child will model the manipulation and domination that the parents are using. They will engage the parent in power struggles, rebel, and withdraw.
- Permissive Parenting causes parents to run out of power because the child's real needs are not met, and challenging behavior will surface as a result.
- Democratic Parenting is about maintaining a connection with your child and making him or her feel included in the process of life's day-to-day activities.
- Democratic Parenting involves communicating with your child in order to solve problems and overcome obstacles. It teaches intelligent thinking, Natural Consequences, self-confidence, self-discipline, responsibility, team spirit, respect, and cooperation.

CHAPTER 3

14 METHODS FOR RAISING HAPPY KIDS

*T*he following is a list of all the points you will learn in this book.

These methods summarize the democratic parenting approach; don't worry, the details of each one are explained in the remainder of this book. This summary can act as your guide and trigger your memory when things get rough. The result is you will be happier, your child will be happier, and you will forge a bond together for life.

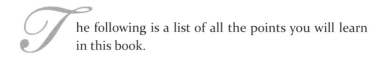

TIP: USE THE NEXT TWO PAGES AS A REFERENCE!

1 **Understanding the 3 Reasons for Misbehavior**
Determine if your child has unmet needs, feels stress, or needs information.

2 **Healing from Hurts and Stress**
Allow your children to heal through their "inborn repair kits" for healing from stress.

3

Natural Giggles

Laughter and giggles are great medicine and create a bond with your child. Find opportunities in your day that allow your child to giggle and laugh with you.

4

Turn Off the TV

Direct your child to another activity instead of watching TV or playing video games.

5

Play Attention Time

Schedule regular time with your children during which you fully listen to them and let them direct the play for a pre-specified period of time.

6

Self-Directed Play

Schedule playtime that allows children to learn, heal, and gain confidence through autonomy.

7

Connective Communication

Talk to your child using kind and gentle words in a considerate, loving, and respectful tone of voice.

8

Limit Setting

Set kind but firm limits to help your children feel supported enough to express their true feelings.

9

Adult-to-Adult Listening Time

Schedule regular time with a friend, relative, or even a support group to have your own feelings listened to. You need an opportunity to connect and dissolve your stress buildup, too!

Family Meetings

Schedule regular time for the family to share appreciations together.

Natural Consequences

Allow your child the opportunity to gain the experience and knowledge that comes from the natural consequence of their choices.

Sugar and Behavior

Ensure that your children eat less sugar, fewer additives, and less fried food. Have them drink more water and eat natural whole foods (raw fruits and vegetables). It's amazing how much diet affects our mood, and, with children, it's even more dramatic. Many behavior issues can be resolved with better nutrition and diet alone.

Exercise Is a Need

Schedule exercise time: kids need to move, sweat, breathe heavily, and push their bodies to explore their limits.

Smart Sleep

Early to bed, early to rise are the habits that lead to easy morning routines and better concentration at school.

"If there is anything that we wish to change in the child, we should first examine it and see whether it is not something that could better be changed in ourselves."

- Carl Jung

CHAPTER 4

3 REASONS FOR CHALLENGING BEHAVIOR

"All children act in annoying, obnoxious, or hurtful ways at times, and they don't always cooperate with our requests. Before dealing with inappropriate behavior in children, it is useful to know why they act the way they do. Once we know this, it is easier to be effective problem-solvers."

- Aletha Solter

In order to practice democratic parenting, we first need to stop ourselves from reacting too quickly to our child's behavior and respond to the root cause underlying it. It's easy to react impulsively when behaviors "trigger" us. We get trapped by the words we use and our tone of voice. Our child's behavior often triggers old, deep-seated memories from our own childhood.

As many a parent has discovered, we often tend to react towards our own kids in the same way that our parents treated us. Even when painful childhood memories made us swear not to be like our parents, we sometimes hear their haunting words come out of our own mouths. These reactions are deeply embedded from our childhood, and they very likely go back some generations. While we also inherit many wonderful family traits and traditions, what we are referring to here is our tendency to react impulsively, and often painfully, when our children trigger us.

Assess First, Respond Second

The first step in democratic parenting is to go beyond the behavior itself, into the underlying reason for its manifestation. We need to focus on the roots, not the fruits. We need to get into the habit of asking ourselves: *"Why is my child behaving this way?"* The more often we ask ourselves this question, the closer we can get to solving challenging behavior.

Trying to fix the behavior with rules, punishments, threats, bribes, negotiations, or rewards is like trimming weeds in your garden. You may not see the weeds after you trim them, but with the roots still in the ground, they will soon pop up again. Even worse, they will multiply. Only by addressing the root-level cause of the behavior will you have the capacity to make life-altering changes.

The first step in *Democratic Parenting* is to understand that there are three reasons for challenging behavior. Whenever your child exhibits challenging behavior, you can use these three reasons as a quick checklist to help you assess the situation and respond intelligently.

We want you to be thinking about, not reacting to, your child's behaviors. Understanding these three reasons puts you into a thinking state so that you can clearly see the simplest way to assist your child.

As you gain an experiential understanding of these three reasons, you will often not need to think about them and will respond automatically to the root cause. Just as it takes time to learn any new skill, it will take you time to develop this one as well and make it a habit. For example, it can take months to learn how to drive a car. When you first got behind the wheel of a car, the number of different things you had to be aware of was almost overwhelming, and the car seemed to be speeding much faster than it actually was.

Yet, after years of practicing driving, you developed the habit of anticipating the flow of traffic, while automatically taking the precautionary measures to avoid any accidents. The process to develop any of the skills in this book is the same; you will anticipate your child's needs, preventing the majority of misbehaviors, while also knowing how to navigate around them when they pop up. Understanding the three possible reasons behind your child's behavior is the most important skill because it gives you access to the root cause of misbehaviors.

1. **Legitimate unmet needs**
    Your child may have a legitimate unmet need, and he or she doesn't know how to let you know about it in any other way. These needs may include the need for attention, affection, social belonging, autonomy, rest, healing, exercise, healthy nutrition, appropriate stimulation, information, participation, growth and learning, or creative expression.

2. **Stress**
    Your child may have an accumulation of unprocessed physical or emotional pressure, tension, or pain, which are forms of stress. Stress, tension, or emotional pressure inhibits a child's ability to think clearly. It's common for children to

exhibit difficult behavior when they are experiencing strong emotions such as fear, anger, resentment, disappointment, confusion, isolation, guilt, or insecurities.

3. **Role models**

Children learn everything through example. They learn how to walk, talk, and relate through modeling the examples in their life. Their first role models are their parents. Siblings, family members, teachers, classmates, and friends are all role models. They all provide examples of behavior, ideas, and characteristics that children may model—for better or worse.

Models for misbehavior often creep in through stories told through books, toys, myths, magazines, and television. As an example: Robin Hood, in the original story, was pompous, rude, violently impulsive, and a rebellious leader of a gang of thieves. Children often act out behaviors they see.

"The art of mothering is to teach the art of living to children."

- Elaine Heffner

3 REASONS FOR CHALLENGING BEHAVIOR

ASK YOURSELF:

"Why is my child behaving this way?"

1. DOES S/HE HAVE AN UNMET NEED?

2. IS S/HE STRESSED, TENSE, OR EMOTIONAL?

3. OR IS S/HE MODELING SOMEONE'S BEHAVIOR
(real or a fictional character)?

Download a free print-out of this page at
www.parentlearningclub.com/3reasons

USING THE 3 REASONS
FOR CHALLENGING BEHAVIOR

Read the examples below and see if you can figure out which of the three reasons is behind the child's behavior. Keep in mind that it may be a combination of reasons. The benefit of this exercise is to get us thinking when our child misbehaves, instead of just reacting.

Scenario Number 1:

One-year-old—dropping food on floor

A one-year-old girl is eating porridge in her high chair. She's noticing the wonderful texture and quality of the porridge between her fingers as well as admiring the bowl. She then picks up the bowl of porridge and turns it upside down, creating a big mess of porridge all over the floor.

Answer:

Given the child's age, we can assume that it's reason number 1—the child is expressing a legitimate need. All children have a need, an inner drive, to explore and learn. Remember that a one-year-old is too young to remember or understand a rule such as *"Don't pour food on the floor."* So, although it's easy to assume that the child needs the rules enforced, we must understand that such a young child cannot be responsible for remembering rules.

Children of this age need to be able to explore the world around them in a safe way. Therefore, **reason number 1, the legitimate need** to explore and learn, even while they eat, is the reason for this behavior. Young children have an interest in seeing things fall and exploring gravity while eating, as well as listening to the sound it makes as it lands on the floor. This is a great reason why we use non-breakable bowls and glasses with children of this age.

You can't fight gravity, and you can't fight this behavior. It will not last forever, but if you suppress this need, your child will get upset and eventually defy you out of needing to find some way to explore and learn. With young children such as this, it's always best to approach it with the attitude of celebrating their innocent development. Just be ready to get messy! Babies, toddlers, and young children will be incessant in exploring their world with creativity and imagination. You should be more worried if they don't throw their food!

Scenario Number 2:

Four-year-old—pushes three-year-old
A four-year-old waits to see that the caregiver is watching and then shoves a three-year-old.

Answer:
Given the child's age, he will know not to shove another child, and, considering the fact that he wanted the caregiver to see him do this, it's clear that he is reaching out to the caregiver for something. The most obvious assumption is that he wants attention. As the old adage goes, *"Bad attention is often better than no attention at all."*

His aggression therefore may be due to **reason number 1, an unmet need**. He may need more attention or fuller attention. Perhaps he just watched two hours of violent cartoons, or maybe an older kid pushed him twenty minutes before when the caregivers weren't watching. He may be feeling tense or stressed and in need of healing, in which case this behavior may be due to **reason number 2—stress**.

Scenario
Number 3:

Three-year-old—tearing up plants in your garden

You've just planted tomatoes in your summer garden, and your three-year-old, who is by your side, starts pulling up the plants.

Answer:

Because of the child's age and, assuming that the child is in a happy state, we can assume that his or her actions are due to **reason number 1, needing information**. A three-year-old would need information about gardening and the reasons for leaving the plants in the ground.

However, if you explained this already to your child and you assessed that she understood it, then she may have another unmet need. Perhaps she has a need to participate and be stimulated more, in which case a three-year-old could easily help you drop seeds into the garden or dig holes for them. By engaging your child in this way, it can meet her need for connection, closeness, and autonomy as well.

Scenario
Number 4:

Ten-year-old—begging & tantrums

Every day after school, your ten-year-old whines, begs, pleads, and throws tantrums until you give him a sugary treat and allow him to play video games.

Answer:

By assessing the state of the child and the desperation and strong feelings behind his need to eat a treat and play video games, we can rightly assume that this habit has become a control pattern to deal with other feelings.

When you assess control patterns, you can take a moment to remember how and when this habit began. In this scenario, let's say that four years ago your child was being bullied at school for some time, so you began giving him treats and let him play video games after school to make him feel better. Four years later, the bullying situation has long been resolved, but the after-school tradition has remained.

Because you've found that your child's behavior gets testy around dinner and at night, you've decided to limit his sugar intake and his video-game time, but your child is testing these new limits by putting up a big fuss.

Because of the strong feelings and desperation in the child's reaction, we can assume that **reason number 2, unresolved stress,** is at work because we can see that we're dealing with an emotional control pattern[5] that distracts the child from other stress or emotions he may be feeling after school.

Scenario Number 5:

Six-year-old boy—violence & aggression
No matter how many times you've lectured, scolded, pleaded with, and punished your six-year-old for hurting his younger sister, he continues to be violent with her.

Answer:
Because we've unsuccessfully tried many disciplinarian methods to stop this aggressive behavior already, we can assume that the reason is not the need for information because the boy obviously knows that he shouldn't hurt his sister. So, in this case we can

---

5 Control patterns are habits or comfort objects that children use to stuff down strong feelings. See Setting Limits Chapter: Limiting Control Patterns to learn more about this.

safely assume that he is acting out aggression due to some unresolved pain, **stress, or tension, reason number 2**.

Yet, often where there is an accumulation of stress or tension, there are also some needs that are going **unmet, reason number 1**. In our assessment, we may discern that additional reasons for his violence are that he needs more affection or full attention.

Scenario Number 6:

Sixteen-year-old boy—school problems & drugs
A sixteen-year-old boy is suspended from school for skipping classes and cheating on tests, while you've found evidence that he is experimenting with drugs.

Answer:
Teenagers who turn to drugs are often lacking the satisfaction of several key **needs, reason number 1**. These are primarily the needs for full attention, social belonging, autonomy, participation, creative expression, appropriate stimulation, and a nurturing environment.

The accumulation of **tension and stress, reason number 2**, is also a major factor. This stress can be due to many things and can build for years before children begin to get into real trouble as teens. As such, it may take time to rebuild the bond and connection with your adolescent child before he begins to open up to you and heal the tension, pain, and stress underneath all his acting out.

In this case, the best approach would be to assess which needs to meet first, while understanding that it may take time, persistence, and patience to rebuild the connection needed for this teen to return to his good judgment and to feel safe, included, and as if he belongs in his school community as a healthy and positive participant.

Working with the school faculty and teachers is vital in this situation to help you discern if there are any problems at school that may cause this behavior. Additionally, by engaging the teachers' help in meeting his needs, you will open the door to a more positive experience at his school.

Consider also the possibility that, in this kind of situation, while you are assessing what the reason for your child's behavior might be, you discover from the mother of one of your child's classmates that the teacher's child is actually bullying your child. In such a case, you will need to speak with the teacher, or even the principal, and you may even need to find another school for your child.

This is an extreme example of a situation where your child's unmet need may actually be a more nurturing school environment. You should take this into consideration when dealing with behavioral issues at school.

Scenario Number 7:

Fourteen-year-old girl—dressing inappropriately
Your fourteen-year-old girl begins dressing very inappropriately by wearing sexually revealing clothing and refuses to eat more than a very small portion of her meals.

Answer:
Reason number 3, role models, is an apparent reason for this inappropriate dress. Let's look at the different examples of role

models that are encouraging this behavior. Firstly, the mother may be the role model for this behavior. Even if she herself doesn't dress in a sexually revealing manner, if the mother buys magazines or watches shows with women dressed like that, the child will follow the mother's interest.

If the mother or other family members don't dress in sexually revealing ways, then we can assume the child is modeling an example of feminine attractiveness outside the family. In our over-advertised culture, the concept of "sex sells" is used to communicate the value of everything from home appliances to personal worth. In a democratic culture, it's the responsibility of all parents to decide if we are to allow our culture to promote anorexic, airbrushed, and half-naked women as examples of womanhood for young girls to follow.

In America, Europe, and in Westernized schools, there is often strong peer pressure for pubescent girls to base their self-esteem on their sexual attractiveness. In this scenario, the girl may also be following the example of her peer group, which has become her role models for her sexuality. Additionally, television shows, entertainment news, and the gossip checkout magazines which target women, continuously spread an unhealthy message about body image and the need to diet. Is it so surprising then that so many teen girls become obsessed with their weight, their diet, and their sexual attractiveness? Girls instinctively follow the example of the women around them.

In addition to **reason number 3, role models**, we also must look to see if she has any **unmet needs, reason number 1**. The most obvious unmet need may be her need for social belonging. This takes us full swing back into cultural and peer role models. Additionally, we can assess that she's learning how to find her identity amidst her changing, pubescent body, and all the hormones and new sexual impulses that happen during puberty. Considering these changes, she may be in need of some extra attention, affection, and information.

One of the best solutions in this case is to focus on her needs for connection, attention, and affection first. That will build a strong connection and may dispel many of these tendencies alone. Your daughter will be more willing to give you information you need or accept your limits if you have a solid, loving connection with her in the first place. Trying to impose limits or fill her need for information with lectures and talks will likely result in more defiance, resentment, and worse behaviors. Fill her deep needs for connection, security, and affection first, and then the doors for real communication will open.

Scenario Number 8:

Eight-year-old with ADHD
Your eight-year-old is having a hard time at school, and the doctor has diagnosed him with attention deficit hyperactivity disorder (ADHD).

Answer:
With ADHD or ADD there are some key **needs, reason number 1,** that we should assess. First is a child's need for healthy nutrition. Children with these issues need to have their eating habits assessed to make sure they aren't consuming too much sugar or refined carbohydrates during the day. Check for gluten or lactose intolerances, or other allergies, which are quite common for these behaviors with kids.

If children don't get enough exercise, they can often become hyperactive and have a hard time staying still and concentrating.

Every child is unique; some will need more exercise than others, but most can usually handle hours and hours of exercise if they're having fun. Modern lethargy from too much time spent watching TV, playing video games, or just sitting in cars and classrooms can easily be fixed through meeting your child's need for more exercise.

Additionally, you should consider the need for full attention. Often when you give children your full attention, their own attention will improve through modeling you. You should consider the need for appropriate stimulation. Both too much and too little stimulation can cause kids to lose interest in just about anything.

Finally, symptoms of ADHD can be associated with **stress, reason number 2**. When children are tense, nervous, or feel emotional pressure, they'll have a hard time paying attention, staying still, and thinking clearly.

"When I was a 5 year old, my mother always told me that happiness was the key to life. When I went to school, they asked me what I wanted to be when I grew up. I wrote down 'happy'. They told me I didn't understand the assignment, and I told them they didn't understand life."

- John Lennon

CHAPTER 5

HEALING FROM HURTS AND STRESS

"Stress is nothing more than a socially acceptable form of mental illness."

- Richard Carlson

$\mathcal{S}$tress—everyone knows what it means, yet it's not so simple to define or to isolate its causes. In fact, there are varying opinions and definitions of stress within the educational, scientific, and medical communities, and all of them point to excessive "pressure" or "tension" creating stress.

Parenting a child is a big enough pressure on good days. However, some days, you may question your child's behavior using the 3 *Reasons for Misbehavior* template and discover that **Reason Number 2, stress,** is at play—so what do you do? In this chapter, you'll discover how to help your child heal the stress and make a radical, practically instant shift into clear thinking and good judgment. Let's first take a closer look at the definition of stress.

From the moment we are born, life makes demands of our senses through various external stimuli. The force of the stimuli exerts a pressure onto us, which we feel as tension. The more connected we are with the situation, and consequently aligned with the stimuli, the more efficiently the pressure is processed and the tension is diffused.

The more we resist the pressure, the more it accumulates. As the pressure increases, the tension builds and morphs into what we call stress. Accumulated stress catalyzes inner chemical friction that can lead to inflammatory build up and toxic hormone overload if it isn't healed.

4 MAIN SOURCES OF STRESS:

1. Aggressive stress: Tangible pain or the fear of pain

- Hitting
- Spanking
- Shaking
- Yelling
- Scolding
- Being a strict disciplinarian
- Abuse:
  - Emotional
  - Physical
  - Sexual

2. Passive stress: The pressure of unmet needs

- Over-stimulation
- Under-stimulation
- No clear limits, boundaries, or direction
- Unhealthy foods and drinks
- Television and video games
- Not enough rest and sleep
- Not enough exercise

3. Situational stress: Challenges beyond your control

- Life changes that are nobody's fault
- Natural disasters
- Divorce
- Hearing about wars
- Accidents
- Diseases
- Death of a family member
- Moving to a new home
- Change of schools

4. Birth stress: The child's stress from being born

- Problems that occur before, during, or after birth
- Fetal or maternal distress
- Prolonged labor
- Traumatic birth
- Early infancy trauma
- Medical intervention during labor (medication, surgery, mechanical birthing device)
- Birth defects

Understanding these sources of stress helps us in two ways. Firstly, it helps us avoid them. Secondly, it helps us heal from the stress. To understand how to heal stress, let's return to our definition:

Stress is the accumulation of unprocessed pressure. Four sources cause this pressure, which we've defined as aggressive stress, passive stress, situational stress, and birth stress. The force of these causes exerts a pressure onto the child that is felt as tension. If the tension is not processed, it will accumulate into stress. At any time, processing the pressure and diffusing tension will dissolve stress. This is what we call "healing from stress."

Stress overrides a children's real intelligence and freezes their ability to be resourceful, flexible, zestful, focused, bright, and situation-centered. Situation-centered means that one's attention and energy is centered on the needs of the situation, rather than on one's own self-centered needs. Children will simply be unable to be situation-centered until their own needs are met. One of our basic needs is the need to heal. That includes healing from physical injuries as well as emotional stress.

8 ways to heal from stress:

Talking about our problems
This is the most mental of stress releases—it allows us to free our mind of the issue by sharing it. It's amazing how much expressing ourselves helps.

Crying
Crying allows the diaphragm muscle to contract and release. Tears release chemicals that both rid our body of the biochemical reaction created by stress and release endorphins to relieve the pain of the stress. Crying has amazing healing properties. Even worse, withholding your tears has negative effects and adds stress to your body.

Symbolic play
Symbolic play is when children "act out" the experience they had that caused the stress. For example, if a child is yelled at, she may in turn make one of her dolls "yell" at another, or, if a television program over-stimulated her, she may need to act out what she saw.

Laughter
We discuss the benefit of laughter at length in the "Natural Giggles" section.

Sleeping

5

Sleeping allows the entire body to relax and rejuvenate. During sleep, the cells are very active inside the body, the immune system is busily repairing itself, and the entire body is in a regenerative state. Sleeping is the body's healing time.

Sweating

6

Sweating flushes toxins and stress hormones out of the body. Some kids and people will spontaneously sweat when stressed; this is the body's natural defense at work.

Exercise and muscle release

7

Exercise allows for heavy breathing, increased cardiovascular flow, and sweating, all of which boost the cleansing system of the body and bring rich oxygen to cells to clear away the stress.

People often respond to stress by tensing certain muscles in their bodies, such as in their shoulders or necks. In addition, if you go through a lot of stress, nothing feels better than a good massage because much of the built-up lactic acid and stress hormones that were freezing up your muscles are released and squeezed out. The muscles are also squeezed, contracted, and released during exercise, which allows them to relax.

You've probably experienced twitches just as you're falling asleep. Children will also twitch when they sleep. This is another way that the muscles and nervous system release tension and stress from the body.

***Getting sick*[6]**

A singular, stressful incident or becoming "run down" by stress can often cause illness. Fevers, colds, fatigue, vomiting, diarrhea, runny noses—these are all natural ways for the body to expel toxins, stress hormones, and, of course, bacteria and other bugs that can come with getting sick.

"Do not suppress it-that would hurt you inside. Do not express it-this would not only hurt you inside, it would cause ripples in your surroundings. What you do is transform it."

- Peace Pilgrim

---

6 Make sure you consult your medical authority when your child is ill.

The healing power of crying

A biochemist by the name of William Frey II studied the chemical makeup of human tears. He wanted to know why humans cry emotional tears as opposed to tears from physical pain. Therefore, for his research study, he had people cry for him and then collected their tears in order to analyze them. The results are highlighted in his book *Crying: The Mystery of Tears*.[7]

He had the adults in his study attend a sad movie, and, as they cried while watching the movie, the participants collected their tears in a test tube. He then had the same group of adults put their faces above a bowl of onions until they cried, and he collected their irritant-induced tears.

He proceeded to analyze these two types of tears—emotionally and physically induced—for their chemical composition. In the emotionally induced tears, Dr. Frey found the hormone ACTH, one of the best indicators of stress in the body.

In his book, Dr. Frey also describes how he had his three hundred research participants, both men and women, keep journals. He had them record the intensity of emotions they experienced, with one hundred being the most intense emotions of sadness, anger, frustration, fear, anxiety, etc. Frey's study indicates that even after shedding just a few tears, participants averaged a 40 percent reduction in the intensity of their feelings of sadness and anger. He also noted that the participants in his research study said they felt happier after crying.

Dr. Frey's research[8] results correspond with many recent studies on emotions, as well as our own experience with adults and children, all of which come to the same conclusion: that people feel better after a good cry.

---

7 We wish to thank biochemist Dr. William Frey II, whose work on tears and whose book *Crying: The Mystery of Tears* are integrated into this section and promoted and encouraged by the Parent Learning Club.
8 (Frey II, 1985)

Babies and young children will naturally cry and rage (hard crying) after a build-up of stress takes place. This is why babies will cry often—not only to let us know that they need something, but also to reduce the stress from the myriad of experiences they have that overwhelm them and are hard to process.

Keep in mind that babies, and even kids, have very limited ways to express themselves. They don't have the experience to understand various stimuli. What to us is normal (a TV program), to a baby might be an awful experience. In addition, babies and kids don't have the vocabulary and general communication skills to express themselves. Especially with babies, the only way for them to express any sort of stress is through crying.

Example of how a baby will release tension through tears:

A six-month-old baby is at the mall and becomes easily over-stimulated by all the sounds, movements, and action around him, and thus begins to cry for no apparent reason. However, as it turns out, the crying will help him deal with the emotional burden of being over-stimulated.

You will notice after a long and good cry that babies and young children return to their natural state of "connection" with themselves, others, and the world around them. They are then relaxed and content, having returned to their curious learning state, taking in information from the environment very rapidly as a six-month-old child will do. This is why we say that children are experts on tension release and on using their natural inborn repair kits to heal from stress.

The chemistry behind the healing powers of tears

Before reading this, you may have wondered why humans cry emotional tears, as Dr. William Frey II[9] did. Only now are

---

9 (Frey II, 1985)

we beginning to understand this remarkable phenomenon and appreciate more the human capacity to work through and overcome stressful experiences. One of the foundational precepts of our parenting system is that tears and crying are an important means for healing from stress.

We want to share with you some of the recent research on the effects that stress has on our hormonal system that, over time, would have a negative effect on the part of the brain that is involved with thinking and memory. This complex physiological formula is explained as simply as possible so that you will see why it's so important for you to help your children minimize and release stress from their bodies. Since we all have to contend with stress throughout our lives, the information you will learn will help your children both now and throughout their lifetimes.

When a stressful event occurs, our body responds with a surge of activity. This is known as the "fight or flight" response, which is an inborn, adrenaline-inducing reaction. This reaction gives us jolts of energy in order to fight an impending danger or run from it (flight). This was a very useful reaction for the early survival of the human species, back when we had to contend with hungry tigers and other predators. Even though we've evolved and live in relative peace compared to thousands of years ago, fight or flight is still an automatic response that happens whenever we experience significant stress.

Physiologically, what happens is that our hypothalamic-pituitary-adrenal systems are activated to secrete glucocorticoid hormones (such as cortisol) that help us during such stressful events. After we have handled the stressful event, the secretion of these chemicals is reduced and then stops.

However, if the event is highly stressful or traumatic, or if the stressful event occurs repeatedly, these glucocorticoids can over-secrete or continue to secrete even after the event has stopped. As a result, they may cause glucocorticoid neurotoxicity, causing neuron-death in the hippocampus. The hippocampus is where memory and learning take place in our brain.

Thanks to many modern studies, it is now known that even hearing about shocking or traumatic events and replaying them in our minds can also cause our hypothalamic-pituitary-adrenal axis to secrete these stress hormones. This can also happen even though we have not directly experienced it ourselves in the moment, such as when watching a horror movie on TV. At times, the re-enactment of these stressful events in our brain can even cause the over-secretion of glucocorticoid hormones that can lead to neuron death.

We know from Dr. Frey's research that people have a reduction in the intensity of strong feelings of sadness and anger—and often even feel happy—after a good cry, which means that after crying, the potential for our adrenal gland to over-secrete glucocorticoids (cortisol) is reduced. In fact, after crying and draining the stressful feelings, it is likely that the over-secretion that is so toxic to our brain is halted. *The glucocorticoid hypothesis of brain aging proposes that exposure of brain cells to glucocorticoids can increase brain cell loss during aging." – Landfield, P.*[10]

Thus, supporting our children and listening to their tears and tantrums return them to a thinking state and a feeling of connection and can likely halt the over-secretion of the stress hormone glucocorticoid (cortisol).

Crying will not only reduce the cortisol in a child's body, but also improves the child's focus and ability to concentrate and respond to you from a state of clarity. This is important because reducing cortisol levels has been found to reduce or eliminate the symptoms of ADD, ADHD and ODD.

---

10 (Landfield, 1990)

Are you preventing your child from healing through distractions?

Here are some ways parents distract their children from crying:
- Offering sweets, food, or breastfeeding
- Rocking or bouncing the child
- Telling them to be quiet or shushing them
- Giving them a soother, pacifier, or comfort object
- Reasoning with them, or distracting them
- Raising your voice or talking in a harsh tone
- Giving them a toy, stuffed animal, or blanket
- Using other punishment or threats

These are just a few ways to distract or repress your child from expressing his or her feelings. Once you've identified the ways in which you distract your child from crying, stop relying on these tactics and allow your child to cry as much as needed. A little crying now is much better than obnoxious behavior later.

Obviously, this list represents kids between the ages of zero to twelve years old. However, remember that children, from toddlers to pre-teens, also need to cry to release their tension. This is true for BOTH girls and boys as they get older.

We understand there are many social pressures that prevent us from allowing our child to cry, but there are ways to diminish stress before going to public places. For example, if your children go to daycare or school, you should spend extra play and connection time with them at home. Often children thrive best by having patterns of activity and passivity, so, after a busy day, it's good to spend some quiet time at home. This gives your child time to relax, reflect, and reintegrate after a stimulating time of activities and social interactions.

If feelings come up and your child wants to release through tears, it's a lot easier to focus and listen at home than in a grocery store where everyone is staring. To avoid these outbursts, take some

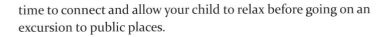
time to connect and allow your child to relax before going on an excursion to public places.

A note about crying in public areas:

If your child does need to cry in a grocery store, it's sometimes easier to stop shopping and take the time to bring her out to the car to finish crying. Of course, it isn't always possible to leave the situation—it may be necessary sometimes to distract them temporarily until you have the opportunity to connect and listen. But make sure you do it! Otherwise, the stress will accumulate and will be worse the next time.

How Do You Distract Your Child from Crying?

Follow this exercise to see how these principles actually work:

First, take out a pen and a blank piece of paper. Sit down and give yourself five minutes of undisrupted time to think. Write down all the ways in which you distract your child from crying using the list mentioned earlier.

You are going to discover something very important about yourself with this exercise. This list will reflect the techniques you use to repress your child's feelings. It's important to write these down so that you will have a clear list of things you do habitually that you may not have realized are harmful for your child's emotional health.

If you've repeatedly distracted your child away from crying, we can assure you that this is one of the reasons why you are dealing with your child's challenging behavior. Luckily, you'll soon learn that if you listen consistently to your child's feelings, the challenging behaviors will melt away.

Important Points:

- We often distract our children from their feelings with sweets, toys, pacifiers, rocking, activities, television, movies, etc., just to stop the tears. It's important to identify these distractions to ensure we adjust our behavior accordingly.

- Realize that typically your child's obnoxious behavior has been building up over a few years, so it's unrealistic to think that it will change overnight. Behaviors and habits take time to change. Luckily, children change and learn much faster than adults do.

- Allow your children to use their inherent repair kits to heal their own stresses: talking, crying, symbolic play, laughter, sleeping, sweating, and exercise.

"The only thing the world really needs is for every child to grow up in happiness."

- Chief Dan George

CHAPTER 6

NATURAL GIGGLES

"What soap is to the body, laughter is to the soul."
- Yiddish Proverb

*N*atural Giggles is a tool you can use on a daily basis with your child to help get back to a state of clear thinking, connected, and present. (We sometimes refer to this as "getting them back on track.") Laughter is an instant connector. Whenever we laugh with someone, we have instant rapport with him or her. Because of this, laughter is an extraordinary stress relief for both children and adults. It's no wonder that it has been called "the best medicine" throughout history.

Laughter is also a sign of connection between you and your child, as well as an indication that your child is enjoying life. Research indicates that children spontaneously have as many as 150 incidences of easy, fun laughter during the day. Using Natural Giggles will remove much of the stress-related tension that your child has accumulated and/or is currently experiencing.

Natural Giggles allows you to:
- Instantly connect with your child
- Help ease the tension of a stressful situation
- Stimulate healing of emotional hurts

"Laughter is the shortest distance between two people."
- Victor Borge

We wanted to provide you with this Natural Giggles skill early in the book because it's a profoundly beneficial and easy means for deepening your connection with your child through play while simultaneously helping him relieve any built-up tension and stress that may be the cause of his challenging behavior. And it is also fun for everyone!

It's easy to do—try it out as soon as you finish reading this chapter! You will be amazed at the instant results.

How to Play "Natural Giggles" With Your Child

You can achieve Natural Giggles in many ways. The goal is to make your child break out laughing. Based on your child's age, she will laugh at different things. Babies will often laugh at a funny facial expression or a big smile. Below are some examples we use which work nearly every time with kids of all ages. If raised with a good sense of humor, even teens will laugh quite easily with these techniques although if a considerable amount of tension exists, or if your child needs to talk something out, then it might take different approaches before you can get her laughing and giggling. The key is to be flexible, keep your heart set on being light-hearted, and enjoy yourself while being very sensitive to your child's responses and state of being.

Befuddled Giggles

One of the easiest ways to make a child laugh is through playacting. All you have to do is play a "fool" or behave clown-like. Pretend as if you are inept or befuddled by something. For example, you can pretend to bump into a chair, and then look confused that you can't get by it. Try to walk again, and each time look more confused. The simpler the action and more confused you behave, the more likely the child will burst out in Natural Giggles.

Funny Voice

Use a funny voice to make simple statements. You can combine the clown-like befuddled act with it—like pretending to be an absent-minded professor. This works great in the car. You can say pretty much anything; for example, read the signs as they pass by—as long as you use a funny tone of voice or accent. You can use this voice to read a book you've read a hundred times in a funny, new way.

With both of these examples, you can adopt a character that your kids will grow to love. Every time they hear and see you take on your Natural Giggles personality, their laughter and smiles will be influenced by the memories of past performances as well as the new one. You may repeat this action as often as you like. Amazingly, children rarely tire of it.

In Natural Giggles, let your child take the role of the more powerful character in the play, while you act less competent and inept enough to enjoy the laughter.

> "At the height of laughter, the universe is flung into a
> kaleidoscope of new possibilities."
>
> - Jean Houston

Using "Natural Giggles" to Help with Sibling Rivalry

After you have grown comfortable using Natural Giggles with one child and understand the principles, you can engage in this play with two or more of your children at the same time. One of the benefits in providing Natural Giggles to more than one child at a time is that it is a very effective way to help children work through sibling rivalry. You practice it in a way that is similar to how Natural Giggles works with one child: you take the less competent role in a light tone of voice, giving your children the upper hand in the play, enjoying giggling and laughing.

When your children are together in the course of play, they may invite you to take the less competent role in the play. If they don't make a direct invitation, you may look for the moment in the play where you can do this, checking to see if they begin to giggle. If the giggles begin, repeat and continue the play with your children.

This allows your children to act cooperatively, and they feel emotionally connected to you and each other without realizing it. It's up to you to ensure you balance your time, attention, and reaction equally among the children so that they all feel a contribution to whatever Natural Giggles game you are playing.

Befuddled Hide and Seek
This game is a modification of the classic game "Hide and Seek." You play the game with one person being "it" while the other

children hide. The person who is "it" counts to a certain number then has to find the hidden children. When you are "it," when it's your time to look for the children or your child, you act slightly inept and befuddled.

Even though you may know where your child is hiding, act confused and slightly bewildered. As you keep looking here and there for your child, your behavior will likely trigger gales of laughter. Start to look in ridiculous places, like in a shoe, or in the garbage can. It is likely that your child will request that you play this game repeatedly because it is fun for them to laugh and creates a warm connection between the two of you.

Ball Keep Away

The children work together to keep the ball from you as they throw it back and forth, and you can't quite catch up with them, nor get the ball from them. All the time you want to exaggerate your ineptness in a light, clown-like way.

Chase

The children want you to run after them, but you can't quite keep up. Then you fall down in a slightly exaggerated fashion as they continue to get away from you. You can act frustrated, exaggerate exhaustion, and so on to make the game fun.

Your children will laugh and giggle at the sheer fun of this light connective play. It will increase their bond as siblings, and, because the play increases their individual feelings that "life is good," you'll see an overall new and improved bond and democratic attitude.

Often, when this play is **repeated consistently**, siblings will begin to naturally support each other in generous, surprising, and considerate ways. As long as you, as the parent, exemplify this attitude, your children will follow when they feel a strong sense of connection.

Using Natural Giggles with your children can be transformational for their relationship with each other and within the family.

A note about tickling:

Natural Giggles is a creative and fun time of laughter for your child. We don't recommend tickling as a means to bring about laughter with your child because it can be invasive. Often children want the tickling to stop before they tell us so. Although there is no ill intent behind tickling, it can in fact cause a child to build up more tension and make him feel powerless.

"So many tangles in life are ultimately hopeless that we have no appropriate sword other than laughter."
- Gordon W. Allport

CHAPTER 7

TURN OFF THE TV

> *"TV rots the senses in the head!*
> *It kills the imagination dead!*
> *It clogs and clutters the mind!*
> *It makes a child so dull and blind.*
> *He can no longer understand a fantasy, a fairyland!*
> *His brain becomes as soft as cheese!*
> *His powers of thinking rust and freeze!"*
> *- Charlie and the Chocolate Factory, Roald Dahl*

Television is an easy distraction: put on a movie and your kids might sit quietly for hours. However, TV can do more harm than good.

The *National Television Violence Study* conducted in the United States found that children's TV programs show up to thirty violent acts per hour. That's three times MORE violence per hour as adult programming! The 2006 Parents Television study *Wolves in Sheep's Clothing: A Content Analysis of Children's Television* found that shows on broadcast and non-premium cable TV channels geared toward five- to ten-year-olds show 7.86 violent incidents per hour.

Violence is not the only form of aggression on TV. Indirect aggression (e.g., gossiping, spreading rumors, and social exclusion) has also been found in kids' movies at rates that exceed the current violence levels on TV. A study showed that Disney films model examples of indirect aggression 9.23 times per hour.

Adult shows with violence, swearing, and sexual content are now being produced in media traditionally reserved for kids. For instance, there are adult-oriented cartoon shows that kids are often exposed to (*The Simpsons, Drawn Together, South Park*), adult-oriented puppet shows (*MAD TV* skits) and pornographic cartoons (Japanese *hentai*). Kids can easily mistake these shows as programming intended for them.

Wrestling shows, which appeal heavily to elementary boys, show thirty verbally aggressive and twenty-two physically aggressive interactions per hour on average, most of which seem to be motivated by nothing else but amusement and anger.

So What Are Your Kids Really Getting from TV?

Nielsen statistics for 2005 reveal that ABC's *Desperate Housewives* was rated the most popular broadcast network show among nine- to twelve-year-olds. Fox's *The O.C.* was found to be very popular with twelve- to seventeen-year-olds. Both shows regularly featured sexually explicit content.

Shows filled with violent themes also ranked highly with teens. These shows included CBS's *CSI* franchise, HBO's *The Sopranos* and FX's *The Shield.*

Although these numbers were from 2005, they were validated in a more recent 2009 study on how teens use media. Many of these shows are still airing today, either as new seasons or as re-runs. Local and cable stations also churn out these shows on a regular basis. Our kids are being bludgeoned by inappropriate content on a daily basis.

Kids See. Kids Do.

It doesn't take much imagination to realize how inappropriate content on television will affect our children. What we see and what we hear become imprinted in our minds. Even if we aren't paying deliberate or full attention, our conscious and subconscious minds are constantly absorbing all kinds of information.

This is illustrated by the way we can surprise ourselves with information we didn't think we had stored. We find ourselves humming the lyrics to a song that was playing on the radio at a restaurant; we know the answer to a quiz question we don't remember learning, and so on. So many things are being constantly stored in our memories without us being fully conscious of it.

The problem with TV programming is that a great deal of it is either misinformation—which is too confusing for children to process—or too far from children's reality and experience, which also makes it hard for them to process.

At times, children will recycle the misinformation from TV viewing just as they may recycle any other emotional hurt, and this can cause them to begin to display challenging behavior. Any kindergarten or school teacher will tell you how children enjoy "acting out" their favorite TV show and characters. Unfortunately, the vast majority of TV shows for children has violent and aggressive characters in the programming, which children then model and mimic.

The Link Between TV and Negative Behavior

As early as 1987, researchers Peter A. Williamson and Steven B. Silvern raised concerns about the effects of violence in media on young kids. In their study of four- to six-year-old kids, they found that instances of aggressive behavior increased among kids who watched violent cartoons and played violent computer games. A previous study in 1986 found that the effects of violent video games are greater than the effects of second-hand tobacco smoke. Not only did violent video games influence IQ scores, but also negatively affected the body's calcium intake system to develop strong bone mass during childhood development.

Boys seem to be particularly at risk for increased violent behavior due to video games. Elementary school boys tend to engage in violent conduct and schoolyard fights that imitate behaviors seen in professional wrestling. Even more alarming, new research shows significant correlations between the time young men spend watching wrestling and self-reports of carrying weapons to school, fighting in and out of school, and physically abusing a date or girlfriend. An English study on how computer games affected teenagers found that in adolescents, aggression increased with total exposure to video games—especially for boys.

However, L. Rowell Huesmann, et al.[11] showed that exposure to media violence at an early age is related to aggressive and criminal behavior for both males and females fifteen years later.

Do Children Know Right from Wrong?

You may be thinking, "But surely when our kids watch TV they can judge for themselves what's right and wrong?" The answer to that question is not simple. Sure, in some situations they can. When it comes to modern media, you need to understand that your child cannot filter out every daily negative message; there are just too many distractions, and the negative message is often too seductively pervasive to stop at every turn.

Biology is against you. Are you aware that when we watch TV for extended periods, our minds and bodies are in a highly suggestible sleep-like state? Because we're "being entertained," our brain's natural defense mechanisms slow down; therefore, the brain temporarily shuts down its logic and analysis so that we can "sit back and enjoy the show." Thus, very little of what we watch is actively analyzed and processed.

In order to raise self-confident kids who can remain healthy and happy through life's challenges and choices, parents need to teach their kids emotional intelligence and appropriate responses to situations. In reacting to a bully, for example, a child needs the capacity to cope with fear and anger appropriately so that he can respond to the bully in a responsible fashion. Excessive TV viewing, however, is not conducive to learning self-control.

---

11 (Huesmann, Lagerspetz, & Leonard, 1984)

TV is addictive. When you watch TV or play computer games, your brain releases endorphins, which are chemicals that make you feel good and relaxed. This makes TV an appealing way to handle frustration and pain. TV is commonly used as a means to repress or push down feelings because television often works as a "control pattern." See the Limit Setting chapter to learn more about "control patterns."

If your child turns to the TV for soothing when upset, you'll never realize the extent of his/her anxieties. Consequently, you won't get the opportunity to react assertively to problems. The results are repressed negative feelings and/or destructive and distracted expression of those feelings.

Lastly, TV can make your child insensitive to other people's pain. Research has found that TV violence leads kids to be less sensitive or sympathetic to victims (Huesmann, Lagerspetz, & Leonard, 1984). It makes them more accepting of violence in real life.

On July 26, 2000, a Joint Statement on the Impact of Entertainment Violence[12] on Children was signed by presidents of the American Medical Association, the American Academy of Pediatrics, the American Psychological Association, and the American Academy of Child & Adolescent Psychiatry. This statement said, "At this time, well over 1,000 studies . . . point overwhelmingly to a causal connection between media violence and aggressive behavior in some students."

There is nothing wrong with more media exposure as they get older and mature. Moderation with anything is the key to balance and happiness. While they are young, keep limiting

12 (Cook, Kestenbaum, Honaker, Ratcliff Anderson, American Academy of Family Physicians, & American Psychiatric Association, 2000)

their media exposure and it can only have a positive effect on your children. Do art, play games, run outside, forage in nature. Sing. Dance. Bake cookies and indulge in giggling fits.

5 FACTORS
That Influence Your Child to Mimic TV Behavior

Psychologist Albert Bandura discovered these five factors and said that kids are more likely to imitate the negative behavior they see on television if:

1. The negative behavior is shown as humorous—kids then see it as harmless fun.
2. The character is rewarded for negative behavior (and the negative behavior goes unrecognized for what it is)— kids learn that the logical and Natural Consequences for misbehavior can be positive.
3. The negative behavior is portrayed by attractive, likeable characters—kids want to imitate these characters they admire.
4. The negative behavior is shown to be "cool" or to attract admiration and attention within the plot of the show they are watching.
5. The negative behavior is portrayed in a realistic fashion (and what seems more realistic than a "reality show"?)— the illusion of fiction is shattered, and the behavior seems much more accessible.

WHAT'S YOUR CHILD'S TV INFLUENCE SCORE?

In the space below, write down all the TV shows your child watches occasionally or regularly.

Also write down the types of commercials they see.

If you don't know which shows or commercials your child is exposed to, then spend an hour sitting with them watching the programming they choose to watch.

Now, take a moment to consider how many shows had content inappropriate for kids. Mark an "X" next to each show on your list that has inappropriate content.

For your "appropriate" measure, use the criteria below. Inappropriate content has reference to the following:

• Violence

• Aggression

• Disrespect

• Selfish behavior and characters

• Evil characters that are doing "evil" things

• Shows that have very fast screen changes

• Shows that try to make the viewer experience suspense or fear, or become overly emotionally engaged in the survival of the characters

• Shows about children who have unfair or unkind things happen to them

• References to sexual matters or adult jokes and content

• Racist, sexist, or classist intonations, comments, jokes, or references

Mark the list of commercials your child is exposed to in the same way. You should end up with a long list of shows and commercials with an "X" next to any that are inappropriate. Evaluate for yourself what the number of "X" marks means in terms of influencing your child.

CHAPTER 8

SELF-DIRECTED PLAY

"Imagination is more important than knowledge, for
knowledge is limited, whereas imagination embraces
the entire world - stimulating progress, giving birth to
evolution."

- Albert Einstein (who failed 8th grade)

*T*he idea behind Self-Directed Play is simply to allow children to direct their own play by setting up a flexible and safe environment where they can fully explore their potential through play. It is one of the most effective ways for children to strengthen and stretch their "learning muscle."

The older models of learning and teaching approached children as if they were "empty vessels" just waiting to be filled with information. However, this model is simply not an accurate representation of how children learn. Children are continually constructing new knowledge based on how they choose to use and explore their environment and the toys or objects that they use and play with.

Internationally renowned infant educator Magda Gerber, who trained in the Loczy program in Hungary, would often say that children are "self-learners." This is why free play is so valuable for children. Self-directed play can be practiced alone, in a mixed-age group setting, or with a parent who is listening, focused, and practicing "Play Attention Time." Play Attention Time is described in detail in the next chapter. This play provides a rich opportunity for children to grow their experience and capacity very rapidly.

In mixed-age groups, younger children learn from observing and mimicking older children. The older children also benefit by gaining more insight and by learning valuable social skills through assisting younger children. This is why children so frequently enjoy playing with kids a little older than they are, provided their experience at play is not too different from each other.

Dynamic Toys vs. Static Toys

Most commercial, plastic toys are what we call "static toys." These toys have a single use: a plastic car is an example of a static toy because it doesn't have many other uses other than being a plastic car. Dynamic toys are open-ended items that stimulate imagination and creative thinking through their multi-functionality. Scarves, pieces of wood, and balls are examples of dynamic toys that can be easily used for multiple purposes.

A teacher once told us how she brought a simple wooden stick that had a notch carved in one end of it into her class. She said that after a couple of days she had counted eleven different ways this stick was used in the play of the children. Some used it as a magic wand, others as a horse. This is a good example of a dynamic toy.

There are many benefits of dynamic toys:

- They are generally much less expensive than static toys.

- They can be made from recycled or natural materials. (Did you know the cardboard box was inducted into the Toy Hall of Fame in 2005?)

- They are much less visually and emotionally stimulating compared to many of the static toys sold in modern stores.

- They stimulate creativity and learning.

- They stimulate cooperative play with others. (Friends and siblings tend not to fight over dynamic toys like static ones.)

In addition to toys, other items or substances that can be used in play are called "manipulatives," which are objects that can be manipulated by children. Dynamic manipulative toys may be water, sand, starch, flour, plasticine, play dough, clay, pebbles, branches, leaves, acorns, cardboard boxes, painting easels, simple art supplies, logs, pillows, wood blocks, scarves, strings, ropes, paper bags, or pieces of wood (sanded-down to avoid splinters). Simple things that we often find in our own backyards can delight the adventures of a child for years.

Setting Up Self-Directed Play

The first step is to set up a free-play environment. In a free-play environment, children are allowed to explore and use the materials at their own pace. The environment should be child-centered and have the appropriate balance of stimulating features. The free-play area must be uncluttered with plenty of space and completely safe for children to explore their potential.

The children are then given the time and space to play at their own rhythm and pace, following their own inner direction and interest. The atmosphere of the free-play area is "encouragement." This kind of setup allows kids to construct knowledge by building on their previous understanding of how they used the materials yesterday combined with their understanding of how they are using them today.

Additionally, this kind of experience allows children to naturally develop creative problem-solving skills and buoyant positive attitudes towards approaching challenges. It also encourages children to engage themselves in their experiences through the force of their own will, rather than through the entertainment value of static, single-use toys and games.

> *"Never help a child with a task at which he feels he can succeed."*
>
> *- Maria Montessori*

Exploring the World Inside and Out

It's best to set up an uncluttered play environment with simple and natural items and toys. It's best to have dynamic toys that can be used for multiple purposes, stimulating your child's creativity and imagination.

Using natural, wood-worked, non-plastic items are what we recommend: wooden blocks, cloths, flags, felt materials, scarves, and balls are basic dynamic toys. You can also use non-sharp kitchen items that are relatively easy for tiny hands and fingers to handle. How often do your children play with their plates, cups, and spoons? These are all natural dynamic toys to them.

The environment itself can be used as dynamic toys. Examples include pillows, couches, chairs, small tables, and so on. We also recommend you use wooden toys and furniture products that provide a warm natural setting. An example is Community Play Things[13], which is an online store. These toys and structures made of wholesome materials are suitable and recommended for both family use and childcare-related settings.

The bathtub is a great place for Self-Directed Play. Simple plastic food or drink containers can become great dynamic toys for young kids to explore water and gravity in the clean and safe environment of the bathtub. Wading pools, sandboxes, outdoor structures, slides, swings, tree houses, and monkey bars are also great. All of these can be set up to maximize safety, which will give your child the opportunity to go as deeply into the Self-Directed Play as possible.

A Note About Toys:
Remember to keep children safe from items that could be swallowed and cause choking such as very small, sharp, pointed, or breakable toys. Also, keep them away from dangerous chemicals that can be ingested. Remember that younger children put everything in their mouths!

Children are at the Center of the Plan

When setting up the Self-Directed Play area, always keep the children at the center of the plan. Think about how to create a

13 http://www.communityplaythings.com

space that allows for ease of exploring, building, creating, and playing that is fully safe and requires minimal adult supervision. Ask yourself, "Where is my child, developmentally and emotionally?" If your child is still crawling, you may use toddler gates to keep your child in the designated free play area.

For teenagers, you would create an environment similar to what adults use to inspire their creativity. A wonderful way to spend time with your teen is to spend some days, and even weeks, setting up his room and/or playroom to be more suitable to his mature tastes.

With babies and young children, the space should be free of choking hazards such as marbles or small things that they may put into their mouths. Babies explore and perceive the world primarily through their mouths—that's why they want to put everything in them. The free-play area for babies and toddlers should be clean and safe enough that they can freely engage in this sensory experience without having the parents constantly pulling things out of their mouths and giving them negative feedback every time they try to explore in their most natural fashion.

As babies develop, they automatically begin to model adults and older children around them, so they will quickly move away from oral tastings and begin to explore things through their other senses: hands, eyes, ears, noses, and mind. Consider this transition when setting up a Self-Directed Play area for your baby or toddler.

For toddlers or crawlers, the toys should be few and dynamic and should encourage the child's imagination, dexterity, spatial awareness, and physical mobility to flourish.

You'll also want to consider how accessible various toys or manipulatives are. It's recommended to have them easily accessible on shelves, in boxes, or organized "in their place."

By having things "in their place," children will learn to develop respect for cleanliness, and organization. This also helps meet children's needs for security and stability because they know that they will always find their favorite ball in the same place. This will also build your child's self-confidence and self-reliance.

Another benefit to having a place for all the items in the play area is that it will give children the ability to put everything away on their own because they know where everything goes. Children have a strong need to participate in life and within their social environment, so this is another opportunity to help enhance a child's self-confidence, self-reliance, and community-based, situation-centered thinking. Children gain an enormous sense of empowerment and fulfillment when they learn to do things on their own.

To optimize the play area's safety, install soft padding where needed. For example, cover all sharp or dangerous corners and edges in the play area with padded material or remove them altogether so that children don't cut themselves if they fall. The idea is to create an area that allows for ease of running, climbing, jumping, throwing, and even digging. If you have a yard, it is important that you set up a specific area that allows for safe and free outdoor play.

The possibilities of making the space fun for learning and experimenting are endless, but you should structure the area with children's physicality in mind, allowing for their ease of movement. For example, you may set up a play structure outside with age-appropriate slides, swings, and climbing obstacles. For those in urban areas, there are often parks that are set up for self-directed outside play.

Don't underestimate the importance of adult support during Self-Directed Play. Should a child's "experiment" lead to a small fall or similar incident, the adult can help adjust the activity so that it will be safer next time. The adult should also be available to listen to crying and help the child recover emotionally from a fall. Tears are good for dissolving fears that may otherwise remain and limit this young explorer in the future.

> *"Eliminate Criticism and Minimize Mistakes: We spend a great deal of our time with our children, watching to see what they do wrong and immediately hopping on them for it. Our prevailing system of training our children seems to be based on the idea that they must be "trained" out of faults and into virtues.*
>
> *However, anyone who stops to think will realize that we really do follow our noses. If our nose points at mistakes, we arrive just there. If we center our children's attention upon what they do well, express our confidence in their ability, and give them encouragement, the mistakes and faults may die from a lack of feeding."*
>
> *- Rudolf Dreikurs*

Set up the Self-Directed Play based on
2 AGE-APPROPRIATE CRITERIA:

1. Age-Appropriate Environment
This refers to setting up the physical environment for the child based on age and developmental stage. For example, you wouldn't leave small marbles or other choking hazards easily accessible for a young baby to play with, just as you wouldn't use a toddler gate in the Self-Directed Play environment of a nine-year-old. A teenager also will need a completely different environment.

2. Age-Appropriate Stimulation
Find a good balance point between too little and too much stimulation. Children need to be stimulated enough to be inspired to play, grow, learn, and explore the world. They need to feel challenged enough that they're actively engaged in the activity. On the one hand, if the play, situation, or environment is over-stimulating, then the child will get tense and frustrated. On the other hand, if the activity or environment is under-stimulating, then the child will get bored, distracted, and may become whiney and nagging.

As a rule of thumb, keep the area uncluttered and as spacious as possible to ensure that the environment isn't over-stimulating. You'll be able to gauge your child's level of stimulation by how he or she responds to the opportunity to practice Self-Directed Play.

The types of toys and manipulatives that are in the Self-Directed Play environment are important in reaching a stimulation balance. Too much stimulation usually happens with modern, plastic, multi-colored, noise-producing, flashing toys. These kinds of toys tend to distract children away from their Self-Directed Play by getting them caught up in the stimulation of the play object (toy, manipulative, video game).

Modern toys are designed to create fascination and obsession in children so that they will want to buy more of the same brand, series, or type. We see how this is marketed to our kids through ads for more toys on the toy boxes, in the instruction booklets, catalogs, and even on the commercials between kids' shows on TV.

Desire and consumerism is nurtured in children when they end up with an over-abundance of static toys, which is more commonly referred to as "spoiling children." The behavior that "spoiled" children usually exhibit is often a result of being over-stimulated by the sheer number of manipulatives at their disposal. This often becomes a vicious cycle, as the child will opt to nag the parent for new toys rather than play with the excess of toys already in his collection.

Natural Movement

Allowing natural movement is an essential practice in allowing your child to experience the benefits of Self-Directed Play. For infants, natural movement means to simply let them view and move in their world, on their own, while lying on their back. This allows their hands, arms, and legs to have free exploration. Another recommendation for infants is to keep them on our laps when they eat, while we support their sitting up position with our bodies. Once they are physically capable of sitting up without support they may sit in a highchair on their own.

For older children, encouraging natural movement includes not lifting them onto climbing structures. Instead, the focus is to stand close enough to catch them if they fall or slip while we let them climb the structures on their own. Allow them to explore and develop their own strength, balance, and hand-eye coordination. Children love to run, climb, skip, dance, jump, and use their bodies to push themselves to new limits as they explore their agility, flexibility, and strength.

Keep in mind that children don't distinguish between appropriate and inappropriate settings for this type of behavior—we make those social rules up as adults. You must have reasonable boundaries, but at times parents can stretch that too far. Allow your children to explore their physical space if they are not disturbing the environment. The more you allow this physicality, the less misbehavior you will experience. Repressing your children's physical energy is a form of stress and can lead to misbehavior.

Self-Directed Play with Mixed-Age Groups

Mixed-age grouping is a superb, natural learning environment for your children. For seventeen years, Isaac Romano, the contributing editor to *The Happy Child Guide,* ran a small, specialized mixed-age group program for young children between eighteen months and six years of age. Having spent more than fifteen thousand hours with young children, he noted a remarkable social, physical, and intellectual learning that took place when children of different ages had the opportunity for "free play" together. Free play is another name for Self-Directed Play.

Older children love to assist and connect with younger children. Younger children love watching the activity and engaging with older children, as long as the activity is age-appropriate to the younger children. Mixed-age settings where free play is possible will allow children to develop the important skills of participation, cooperation, communication, teamwork, and group problem solving—all of which are vital life skills as children grow into teens and adults. It's in the early years of your child's life, particularly between the ages of eighteen months and six years, that they will develop their basic relationship patterns, communication skills, and teamwork habits. Setting up regular and safe Self-Directed Play for your child will give her foundational life skills and social abilities that will rival the best colleges or universities.

Preventing Sibling Rivalry in Self-Directed Play

If you have siblings that are similar in age, you'll want to set up the Self-Directed Play environment so that there are duplicates of the same toys and manipulatives. By having duplicates for multiple children, there will be less fighting over single objects. This helps prevent having to deal with "sharing" issues because there will be enough manipulatives, toys, or objects for each child to play freely with. Even having multiple toys of the same color helps to avoid these arguments from arising. When you make sure each child has the same toy—color, shape, type, everything— then you'll be preventing a good portion of sibling rivalry.

Important Points:

- Set up the Self-Directed Play environment so that it is fully safe, uncluttered, and has easy access to age-appropriate toys, manipulatives, and objects.

- Tuck away anything that poses a possible hazard for your little one: books, CDs, that special crystal vase, anything that you don't want your child touching or getting into.

- When your child is practicing Self-Directed Play, let him or her "take the lead" in the play. Avoid leading the play yourself and instead just follow the child. Try not to give suggestions or too much stimulatory feedback during the play; just try to follow and encourage the child's own initiative.

- Set up inside and outside free play environments while making the area child-centered, allowing for plenty of natural movement.

- Give your child dynamic, multi-use, and open-ended toys and manipulatives with which to play and explore. Minimize the number of over-stimulating, single-use "static toys."

The greatest sign of success for a teacher... is to be able to say, "The children are now working as if I did not exist."

- Maria Montessori

CHAPTER 9

PLAY ATTENTION TIME

> *"How we treat the child, the child will treat the world."*
> *- Pam Leo, Parent Educator*

*I*n order for your children to have good judgment and enjoy life, it is important for them to feel connected to the world around them. This feeling of connection is very fragile and is easily broken by feelings of isolation, criticism, and by experiences that are difficult for children to process.

So how do you cultivate and then maintain your child's connection to you and the world? The first thing you want to do is to schedule Play Attention into your weekly routine. Making this a priority in your week will yield the most amazing results in both your and your child's life.

What is Play Attention? It is a form of playtime where you give your undivided attention to your child and let him take the lead in the play. During Play Attention Time, you need to make sure you are actively listening to your child. You must listen empathically and pay attention to your child's subtle cues.

How to Practice Play Attention Time

Yes, I know it sounds funny to say we need to "practice" how to play. But what we need to practice is how to *listen effectively*. Let's just be honest with ourselves; even when we're having a conversation with someone we care about, how often are we really and truly listening to the other person? To answer that, let's define what listening means.

Many of the North American Natives tribes used to hold (some still do) a "talking stick" while engaging in a conversation. The premise is simple—whoever holds the stick speaks. But this is not all. The REAL purpose of the talking stick is to draw attention to the speaker so the listeners pay full attention. The "talking stick" is inappropriately named; it should be called "the-pay-full-attention-to-me-stick." The stick is a reminder to the listener to put himself into the speaker's shoes—to truly build a bridge of empathy and get into the speaker's frame of mind. The listeners then ask themselves: Why is the speaker saying what she is saying? What is important to her? What is she feeling? What deep needs and feelings is she expressing?

Now let's be honest again—most of us don't listen to others like this. Often while someone is speaking to us, we are already thinking about our rebuttal, or we are thinking about whether we believe what he says, or we are thinking about what we are going to say next, or we are thinking about how we feel about what he is saying. Maybe we are even waiting for the conversation to end and are daydreaming about what we are going to do next.

You can see that the pattern in these latter examples is not about the speaker but about our own selves. There's nothing empathetic about it. To truly listen, you must connect with the speaker. You must be empathetic to his situation and to his state of being and seek to understand him completely rather than seek to be understood.

We ALL need to practice empathetic listening, especially with our children. Play Attention gives you a dedicated time to build an empathetic bridge to your children and connect with them—without distractions.

So what does giving them your full attention mean? It means that you cannot do two things at once. You cannot cook and be involved in Play Attention Time. You cannot pay your bills, talk on the phone, surf on the net, chat on Facebook, text message, or do any other activity during this time. It is time entirely dedicated to your child.

Believe us, it is a small investment to make for a massive amount of return. When practiced regularly, it's like making deposits into your family's emotional bank account because you'll be fulfilling at least two of your children's most fundamental needs—the need for connection and the need for autonomy (which is fulfilled by allowing them to direct the pace and type of play).

Your child will really soak up this time, as it deepens his or her feelings of love, trust, and safety. If your child is emotionally hurt or stressed in some way, Play Attention is crucial in creating a safe time where your child can really open up and dissolve stress. Also during Play Attention Time, he or she may express an anxiety, issue, fear, insecurity, or other feeling that he or she may not otherwise have disclosed to you.

So how do we do this? First we set up the environment and have the time and space to allow us to be engaged with our children without distractions. Start by scheduling at least two, preferably three to four, Play Attention sessions during the week. Each session could last sixty to ninety minutes. One hour of full attention is a good amount to schedule for this activity when you start. Eventually, you'll discover what is best.

You may enjoy doing more Play Attention, and you may be able to satisfy your child's need for full attention with less time, while certain situations require longer periods. For example: after a stressful experience, or if you have been away for a while, busy, or distracted, your child may need more full attention to help him get back on track. One hour is what we have found to be a good place to start, as it will allow you to relax and really be with your child.

Once you can do this, you're 75 percent of the way there. Simply provide your children with actual and real attention, where you truly focus only on them and follow their lead in the play, instead of trying to distract them, entertain them, educate them, inform them, and lecture them.

There are some benefits to this time for you, too, as a parent. You will feel energized, calmer and more connected afterwards. This is a great "stress-free" time for you as well. Just be sure you don't let a day's exhaustion and stresses interfere with this time. You need to give your child a period of full attention and good listening. Therefore, if you are completely exhausted, you may need to recover and rest before engaging in Play Attention.

This type of attention is a deep emotional need, with no middle ground. Imagine you are speaking with someone and telling him about an exciting experience you just had, and then the phone rings and he answers it, ignoring you. How would that make you feel? We've all felt that little sting before. With children, it's an even greater emotional trauma. Moreover, considering how busy and distracting the world is today, we often end up doing this without realizing it. That's why Play Attention is so important.

Let your children direct the play. Let them pick and lead the activity. Let them set the pace and the tone of the play. You may sit quietly and draw together, you may go for a walk, build models, play with blocks, and so on. Playing outside on structures, which puts you in a role of spotter or helper, is also fantastic as it allows your children to push their limits and feel safe. During Play Attention, you may also find great opportunities to play Natural Giggles.

Play Attention does not involve going to a movie, watching TV, or other passive activities that disconnect you from each other by encouraging you to focus on something else. You won't reap the same benefits from these types of activities.

Your activity should allow for the opportunity for your child to communicate with you if she needs to. Often if something is bothering your child at school, at home, or anywhere else, she will begin to share this with you during Play Attention Time. Don't pry or try to force it; just let it come up naturally if your child chooses to discuss it. Simply providing time and space for you and your child to connect can resolve many issues.

If your child does try to communicate an issue or ask a question, or if she begins to feel and act anxious, the attention you're giving your child will allow you to notice those subtle cues so that you can encourage what she is doing or saying. For example, if your child begins to get frustrated with trying to build a toy because it keeps falling down, you can say something like, "Hmm, I wonder how we can make that stable so it doesn't fall down?" In this way, you don't try to solve it for her, nor do you get caught up in her frustration; instead, you help direct her to a solution through your encouragement and belief in her.

Another example is if your child says something like, "It's not fair that I don't get to play video games and the kids at school do." You can respond by saying, "Yeah, I can understand why that would be frustrating." At this point, your child may go in for the sale and say, "So, why don't you let me play video games, Mom?" Here you can simply redirect the conversation away from the superficial issue and bring it closer to the emotional issue by saying, "Sweetie, I'm not going to let you play video games now, but I'm more than happy to listen to your feelings about it."

Persistent children may continuously corner you into making a buying decision around an object such as a video game, a doll, a toy, or clothes, but your role here is to be a listener, so you must continuously reinforce that in your resolve to just be with your child and listen empathetically, without harsh tones. What may happen is that your child will eventually have a cry or a tantrum about these superficial desires that will help him heal from the tension and stress around it.

Listen to everything they have to say and encourage them to share more of their feelings and expand on what they are trying to express. Try to hold back your response, explanation, definitions, defense, reasoning, and so on, and just let them express themselves fully. If your child needs to heal from an emotional hurt or stress through talking, the best thing you can do is just listen empathetically, without adding any logical feedback.

For example, if your child says something like, "I didn't like how you yelled at me the other day." Instead of defending or explaining your reason for the outburst, give an empathetic response like, "I understand that you didn't like that," or "I can see why you didn't like that, and I'm sorry that I lost my patience."

You want to encourage children to express themselves fully, and the more your child feels heard and listened to, the more he will naturally express himself. He needs to feel as if he can say anything to you. This goes miles in building a bond of deep trust with your child so that he can always depend on you, open up to you, and share deeply with you. By establishing this connection with your child, you will virtually rule out the risk of peer pressure in the teen years, as he will come to you when this happens and genuinely seek out your advice and guidance.

When you feel your child has drained the stress and tension around any issue, you can then begin to offer encouragement, love, gratitude, and other positive expressions about her, not about the issue itself. Try to avoid explanations, rationalizations, and defending your or someone else's actions. Also try to avoid platitudes like, "Don't worry, things will get better." It is far better to simply acknowledge the issue and her feelings towards it.

A note about finding solutions:

Good psychologists and counselors often employ these practices in therapy sessions. Counselors rarely provide solutions; they encourage expression, communication, and connection with issues to help release the trauma and anxiety associated with it. It provides a space to heal the heart and mind. Solutions and actions come afterwards, naturally.

Some children will be more communicative than others will. Some may never bring anything up, and that's OK too. The point of Play Attention Time is not to delve into these matters, but to give your child dedicated, focused, uninterrupted attention so that he can replenish his connection to you and the world. It's like filling his gas tank with fuel—Play Attention Time is the fuel pump, and connection and belonging is the fuel. He will drive away strengthened, secure, and happy.

Here are some tips:

Tips on how to establish an empathy bridge to maximize the benefit of Play Attention Time:

- Be present with your child; try not to think of what happened or what's next.

- Let your child lead the play.

- Keep your focus on showing your child how much you love her and how much you enjoy spending time with her.

- Avoid phone calls, text messaging, and other interruptions.

- Avoid multitasking activities such as cooking, doing the laundry, cleaning, paying bills, writing emails, checking Facebook, and other activities.

- Consider this time as also valuable to you for refilling your own emotional gas tank.

- Play Attention is a great way to transition between activities or parts of the day, from school to home for example (and for you from work to home).

When we present Play Attention Time to parents, they sometimes tell us, "Well, we both spend lots of time with our

106

children. Is this Play Attention Time?" There's no denying that you spend a lot of time with your kids and how beneficial that is, but remember the Native talking stick; Play Attention Time is about listening and focusing on your child in an intentional, meaningful way. You may very well be doing Play Attention Time already, but by bringing your focus to its importance, you may now get even more out of it and realize how beneficial it is to you and your child.

Parents today are so often too exhausted, stressed, distracted, overwhelmed, and too busy to really "just be" with their children. Sadly, we lose this precious opportunity to really connect and communicate deeply and meaningfully with our children, due to the hectic lives we lead and the multitasking that life often requires. Play Attention is an effective way to reestablish that connection of trust and love with your children.

You'll find the benefits of Play Attention Time cumulative. The more often you do it consistently, the greater the benefit and the fewer resulting behavior issues you will have with your children.

> *"Children need love, especially when they do not deserve it."*
>
> *- Harold Hulbert*

> "A mother holds her children's hands for a while...their hearts forever."
>
> - *Author Unknown*

Play Attention Time with Multiple Children

Play Attention Time is very effective with two or more children, especially when sibling rivalry is an issue. Fully listening to your children as a cohesive group provides them with the attention they need. This will also demonstrate to them that there is no need to compete for your attention. Often, whatever anxiety, stress, or other issue is causing friction between siblings can erode through regular group Play Attention Time.

If feasible, we would encourage you to have at least an hour or two of Play Attention Time with each of your children separately every week, and then some time with all your children together. This will allow each child to have the opportunity to work through any issues. It will also help create a deeper bond with you, even when there are no issues at hand to work through.

What happens if one child starts crying while others are around?

Allow your child to cry and release feelings. The other children will understand that this is a secure environment and will likely play on their own (Self-Directed Play) while you tend to the crying. Children have an intuitive sense of when the crying is about attention and when it's stress relief, and they will know that during Play Attention Time, crying is rarely about seeking attention.

There are times when one sibling's crying causes a release in others as well—a sort of trickle-down, trigger effect. This is perfectly normal. Simply allow them to have a good cry and don't stop them. Remember, crying is the indication of stress release, so just continue to provide attention and stay close and responsive.

What if You Can't Handle It?

Strong feelings can surface and be drained during Play Attention Time, and a situation may arise where you're feeling unable to listen to the crying and raging of your child, or several children, at the same time. What you may find you need to do in that particular moment is to divert or redirect your children's attention and see if the crying will cease.

Obviously, we don't recommend this as it will postpone the much-needed healing of your child. However, we understand that we all have limits, and sometimes your own emotions are too strong for you to deal with your child's strong feelings at that moment. You may be tired from a long day, feeling ill, or in a bad mood.

There will likely be other times where your children will bring up these feelings that they are attempting to work through. The tantrums may get worse before they get any better if the tears are often repressed and Play Attention Time ends too soon. So, make a plan in your schedule for a moment when your attention is available, so that you may listen to these feelings when you have the emotional fortitude to handle it.

Important Points:

- When practicing "Play Attention Time" and "Natural Giggles," keep it light. Male caregivers and fathers tend to lean on the side of being too loud and over-aggressive in their play. Play attention is not a physically intense playtime—there will be lots of opportunity on other occasions to get rowdy. Remember to keep it vocally, physically, and verbally light. You want to ensure your child maintains the "competent leader" role in the play. This gives them security and confidence to be more open and free in their expression if that's what they need, and it also allows them to meet their need for autonomy, which increases their self-confidence and cooperation.

- Keep the play age-appropriate. Again, we want to avoid complexity, as that will diminish the child's confidence and role of competency we want them to take on.

- Notice the times when your child laughs spontaneously, especially while you're spending Play Attention Time. If she laughs at something you do, do it again. This is a great lead-in to Natural Giggles. Don't underestimate the power of laughter. Laughing and giggling regularly can correct many challenging behaviors. You will be amazed at the results you can get.

- The last thing you want to do is smother your child or exhaust yourself with Play Attention. When you give your children this focused attention, give them space to explore and be the leader in the play. Just listen and respond whenever they engage you. Avoid leading the play or overly engaging your child's interest in something you find interesting. Instead, give him space and let him navigate and explore his environment. If you find yourself feeling drained after Play Attention, you may be leading the play too much. This is a good time to relax into the role. Eventually you will begin to feel energized by Play Attention Time.

"The best inheritance a parent can give his children is a few minutes of his time each day."

> *- Orlando A. Battista*

CHAPTER 10

CONNECTIVE COMMUNICATION

"Encouragement is more important than any other aspect of child-raising. It is so important that the lack of it can be considered the basic cause of misbehavior. A misbehaving child is a discouraged child. Each child needs continuous encouragement just as a plant needs water."

- Rudolf Dreikurs

*C*onnective Communication involves using your words, body language, and tone of voice to create an empathic bridge (connection) with your child. One of the core tenants of *Democratic Parenting* is connection. We've said it before, and we'll say it again—your connection to your children has a greater influence on their well-being than anything else you can do.

We know this is a hard thing for parents to hear sometimes because they try so hard to connect with their children, and they don't feel that this is the issue. They put in the time and effort and have all the love in the world to share with their children, but still they can't get that deep bond. Why is that?

It's because most people don't *communicate* for creating connection. We communicate with our children the way we've seen others do it and the way our parents communicated with us. At times, these can be good models, but, many times, they are not.

Various forms of communication can lead to connection. Through verbal and physical communication we can "reach for" our children when they feel disconnected and maintain a strong and loving sense of connection throughout the day.

In this chapter, we are going to teach you some fundamental communication skills that will help you develop a continuous connection and get your child listening and paying attention to you. As you practice the techniques that we show you in this guide, you'll start to become more aware of the "connected feeling" that you and your child have. You'll notice that when she feels connected, she is more relaxed and cooperative. And as you stay connected with your child, you'll also become aware of how certain words and verbal responses will cause the feeling of connection to break.

Children are hypersensitive to the world around them. They integrate everything they see, everything they smell, everything they hear, and everything they taste into their minds and bodies. They process, memorize, and model these experiences. Children today are also being stimulated at nearly one hundred times the rate of children forty years ago.

Can you imagine the overload this puts on a fresh young mind that doesn't yet have the filters, experience, and emotional capacity to deal with the bombardment of today's world! Children today need a solid and stable connection to hold onto—a safe haven in all this craziness. They count on you for this.

To create a connection with your children:
* Speak to them using kind and gentle words;
* Be extra considerate and patient with them;
* Use a loving and respectful tone of voice. (This is huge for parents speaking with their pre-teens and teenagers!)

Simply put, you need to speak to your child based on where they are emotionally—you have to feel their state of being and respond in a manner that helps bridge a connection. Your child has to feel the empathy and safety of your presence.

If they are scared, you need to be reassuring.
If they are excited, you need to be interested.
If they are angry, you need to be patient.
If they are hyperactive, you need to be concentrated and connect with them calmly.
If they are in a wild tantrum, you need to be extra patient but firm.

Speak with the intention of restoring and strengthening your love and connection with them. Remember that your body language and your tone of voice are *both* major components of communication—usually more so than what you say. Body language and tone are especially important for younger children as they have limited communication capacity and vocabulary to express themselves and to understand you.

When it comes to children, body language also includes height. An adult's stature can comfort a child by providing a feeling of safety. However, to connect with a child or comfort them when they are upset, you need to get down to their level so that they can see you "eye-to-eye."

The final component of communication is your choice of words. Begin to develop your own vocabulary of phrases and words that remind you of the importance communication plays in establishing a connection and the power of that connection. These words will also remind your child as well. Consistent use of vocabulary establishes immediate familiarity and helps bring about a quicker connective feeling in your child.

5 MAGIC WORDS AND PHRASES

The following are five words and phrases we've found to work well. These can help you get started as you develop your own.

"Sweetheart or Sweetie..."
This is just a way of conveying your deep love for your child when you are addressing him. You can also use "Darling," "My love," etc. By using these terms of affection, your child will feel more loved and cared for.

"Not right now..."
This is a gentle alternative to saying "no" when your child asks for something. You can also use this phrase when setting a kind limit when your child reaches for a control pattern. For example, if she asks you to buy some sweets at the grocery store, you can reply, "Not right now, sweetheart."

3 "We" or "Us" (instead of "You")

This is a great way to build a sense of inclusiveness and togetherness. Using "we" instead of "you" also has a tendency to diminish rebelliousness, arguments, and defiance, and to encourage cooperation.

So instead of saying, "It's time for **you** to brush your teeth and get ready for bed," you can say, "**We're** going to brush our teeth and get ready for bed." Or, instead of saying, "**You** need to get ready for school now," you say, "It's time for **us** to get ready for school." If your child makes an excuse or begins to argue, you simply answer, "It's just what **we** do."

You need to make your child feel connected to you and to the family. Using inclusive language will help make your child much more cooperative, as he will feel more "a part of the whole family" and feel less that he is being isolated to do something he doesn't want to do.

For example:

Parent: "It's time for us to go to bed, sweetheart."
Child: "Why do I have to go to bed?"
Parent: "It's just what we do."
Child: "I'm not tired! Just one more hour."
Parent: "Not tonight, sweetie. We don't want to be tired for tomorrow. Let's go to brush our teeth, and we'll tuck you in."

Notice how in this example we stay on topic and on task. We never deviate from the issue at hand. You'll notice we used a consequence in the example. This was not done punitively (i.e., as a threat of punishment); it was done as a natural, factual consequence. We also included "we" in the consequence so that it's not personal because if your child stays up another hour, you too are going to be tired tomorrow!

116

For example:

Parent: "It's time to clean up your room."
Child: "I'm just going to watch one more video first."
Parent: "We can watch another video after we finish cleaning up, sweetie."

Of course you'll want to be reasonable and empathic to the situation. If your son is in the middle of building a model and doesn't want to leave the glue or paint open because it will dry, then that is a reasonable reason to wait a few minutes. In these sorts of cases, it's best if you spend a few minutes helping him finish what he is doing so that he can comfortably move to the next thing. This is a good time to practice Play Attention.

What happens though if your child just sits there and refuses to move? (I'm sure this has happened to you!) Let him. Don't threaten with punishment or bribe with reward. This really only teaches your child that "cleaning up" (brushing teeth, going to bed, or another task) is just what everyone does. By doing this you will be teaching him that this is not an excessive request you are making and not something to fight over. You're turning something that is a chore into an everyday habit.

What you are doing is taking a firm but GENTLE stance. You are setting a "kind" limit. Your child will soon learn that arguing with you or defying you is useless and wastes time and energy. Children are smart—they will discover that cooperating with you is the simplest way for them to get what they want. If they are reasonable, you are reasonable. Isn't that a great habit to cultivate?

4

"That's a great idea, *and* I think..."
This is two parts. The first part, "That's a great idea," is another alternative to saying "no." Often times your child will express

a good idea—or maybe it seems like a good idea to her. By responding with "That's a great idea...," you will be encouraging your child to think. You will also be encouraging her self-confidence and desire to cooperate with you. Furthermore, by responding this way, you are modeling respect. And, because you are respecting your child's thoughts and ideas, she, in turn, will be more likely to respect yours.

By using "and I think" instead of "but," you will avoid negating your child's "good idea." If you simply say, "That's a great idea, but...," you're in essence negating the notion that she had a good idea—the word "but" has a negating effect. So by replying "and I think," you can add to your child's thought and help her see why you'll take a different action from what is suggested.

For example, if your child asks for an ice cream, instead of simply saying, "No, we don't have time now," you can respond, "That's a great idea, honey, and I think that because we're supposed to meet Daddy at home in twenty minutes, we don't have time to get an ice cream today."

Of course he may still protest, nag, and give you rebuttals, but at least by using this language you're keeping the communication channels open to foster a more respectful and connected relationship with your child. You'll notice that over time those rebuttals and protests will become weaker. Trust us though, when it comes to sweets and ice cream, the rebuttals will never go away! But your child will no longer throw tantrums, if he did before, once you start using, "That's a great idea, AND... ."

"I'm right here with you" or "I see you"
This is a simple way to "reach for your child" and help him feel connected to you. You can use this to stop a tantrum before it

starts, or to connect with your child if he is crying or having a tantrum as part of an emotional stress release. Remember, you determine if a tantrum is an emotional release by using the "3 Reasons for Challenging Behavior" to discover the root cause of the behavior. So, you can use this language if your child starts to whine or is having a big release through a tantrum or a cry.

For example:

Your child shouts: "Mommy, mommy, mommy!" from the other room.
You reply: "Yes, sweetheart, I'm right here with you."

In this example, the child is just looking for a quick connection, and this response will usually resolve it. However if he keeps calling for you, there is likely a need that is not being met, and you will need to address this.

Asking Questions

One of the best ways to respond to a child's question, retort, outburst, or other issue is to ask clarifying questions. It's critical to always ask questions to clarify your child's motives. You want to frame your questions in the way that will help you provide the solution to your child's problem.

For example:

You feel your child is lacking affection, but you're not sure. You can ask the following question: *"Do you want mommy to just hold you, or listen to you, or sing to you?"*

If your child responds positively, then this question addresses her true need. If not, then you need to dig further.

For example:

You find your child scratching paint off the wall with a spoon. You can react, or you can ask a clarifying question: *"Sweetie, what are you doing?"*

You might think it's crazy that the kid is scratching paint off the wall! But let's be realistic, the damage is done. Getting angry at this point will get us zero long-term results and will likely have a negative emotional impact.

Let's think about this scenario for a moment. For an adult, chipping paint off the wall with a spoon is an outrageous action, but to the child it's just something to do. She may have noticed part of the paint was peeling and wanted to discover what was behind it. To a young child this is perfectly rational logic. You can likely see where this is going. If you react with anger to this situation, you are teaching the child that curiosity and exploration are bad and will make the people who love you angry at you.

There is even more power in asking the clarifying question—you may discover something fascinating about your child! You can gain incredible insight by asking about children's motivations.

This situation above happened with my son and me. Guess what his answer was? First, he looked at me as if I was asking him a ridiculous question and said, *"I'm taking the snow off my spaceship."*

How many famous authors, movie directors, artists, mathematicians, musicians, scientists, doctors, lawyers, and so on have been children and had such a robust imagination? One day your child may use that imagination to become a doctor, make a creative leap of inspiration, and cure cancer.

Or you can yell at him and end his imagination and creative thinking once and for all.

It's amazing the power we have as parents. My first thought in this scenario, when I saw my son peeling the paint, was that he was just trying to drive me nuts. Seems like a ridiculous reaction— my five-year-old has nothing better to do than provoke me. Sometimes this is true, and children act out to get attention; but even if that were true, yelling at him would not have solved the root cause of the misbehavior, and it would have repeated itself. Instead, I discovered something about my son that day—that he has a gloriously deep and creative imagination.

What did I do then? When I understood the situation, I explained to him that I don't want paint coming off the wall but that I would be happy to provide something else to do of a similar nature. Things that seem absurd to us can be perfectly normal to our children. They're doing something that makes sense to them, but it may not always make sense to us.

Imagine your child at a restaurant. He decides to pour soy sauce into his drinking water. "Uh-oh," you think, "this is going to get messy." You wait to see what's going to happen next, and your child decides to pour the murky water into his bowl. You ask him to pause for a second and ask what he is doing. The response? Eating broccoli. It tastes better when dipped in diluted soy sauce. The same child that wouldn't touch his vegetables discovered a way to eat them that made sense to him.

Yes, this happened to me again. Once again, I offered my son an alternative to pouring the glass into the bowl, and he obliged and went happily back to eating more broccoli than I've ever seen him consume. Not really to my taste, but who am I to judge his taste buds!

Instead of assuming that your child is purposely making a mess or bothering you, stop and ask a question first. You may be surprised at what she tells you. You will gain insight into her motives. Children have wild and vivid imaginations. The more we understand and respect our children, the more they will respect us, and, in turn, become more cooperative.

We've seen this work for countless families who've used this approach. The more children are given space and respect, the more they want to help.

Try this out the next time your child does something that upsets you:

- First, empathize with your child and practice "**non-reaction.**"

- Then ask her what she's doing.

- Once she tells you what she's up to, try to understand what she's doing from her point of view.

- From here on now, you can offer her an alternative that respects her logic and imagination, while explaining that her current pursuit has a negative impact (it will make a mess, etc.).

- Finally, pay close attention to see if she acts differently in the future—you will likely begin to notice she makes better and better decisions.

What If My Child Is Too Young or Doesn't Answer Me?

If your child is four or under, here's something to keep top of mind. Everything your child does is out of pure innocence and zest. He is not doing it to upset you. He is simply too young to formulate that level of thinking. He may try to get your attention by defying you, but he is not deliberately trying to hurt you. With that consideration, you can connect and proceed with all the above examples.

What If My Child Ignores Me?

If your child blatantly ignores you or doesn't want to speak with you about what they are doing, that's OK. Ask him again and explain to him what's going on for you.

For example:

"Mommy is wondering what you're doing. I'm concerned about the paint on the carpet. Could you tell me what your idea is so that I can better understand and help you?"

You see, most children are used to being punished, so they will hide what they are doing at all costs. If you have punished your child before, it may take some time to get her to communicate openly with you without being afraid of punishment. If you want to have a cooperative and respectful relationship with your child, you need to teach your child that it's safe for her to be open and honest with you, even when she makes mistakes. *Especially* when she makes mistakes!

She needs to know it's safe to trust you. Have patience while you practice this with your child, and be persistent. Let her know that she can trust you and that you want to understand her. Remember, authoritarian punishment may make the child "behave" in the short term, but the long-term effects of this may backfire. Let's review what we learned at the beginning of the book:

"Children from authoritarian parenting lack social competence as the parent generally predicts what the child should do instead of allowing the child to choose by him or herself. The children also rarely take initiative. They are socially withdrawn and look to others to decide what's right. These children lack spontaneity and lack curiosity."

"These children are often the most vulnerable to enter into relationships with or marry equally abusive and controlling partners or develop mental illness when they enter adulthood. (Although arguably this may be genetic as mental illness sometimes might be the reason behind some of the more extreme cases of authoritarian parents.)"

"Some children might also rebel by openly defying the parents by leaving home at a younger age, partaking in drugs, alcohol, and sexual behavior at a much younger age than some of their peers as well, dating and/or marrying a partner whom they know their parents would disapprove of, and often might be estranged from their parents during adulthood."

Offer an Alternative

The best part about transforming your child from exhibiting defiant, out-of-control behavior to being respectful and cooperative is that you have less cleaning to do! It's true, by having a cooperative child you can significantly reduce the mess you have to clean up every day. And if you're like most busy parents, that's a pretty big bonus!

One very effective alternative to punishment that helps boost your child's self-esteem is to offer an alternative. It's important to remember that your child wants to explore the world, and she needs space in order to do that. At the same time, however, you don't want a mess everywhere, so here's a great way to create a "win-win" situation for you and your child. If your toddler is exploring the effects of gravity by pouring milk on the floor, before reacting, first take a moment to **evaluate** the situation. Then consider *offering your child an alternative.*

For your child who is exploring gravity by throwing food on the floor, water in the sink would be one alternative, playing outside with the hose would be another. There's no point in punishing your child with harsh words, which only fosters low self-esteem. Instead, there are many alternatives.

We know that non-reaction can be a challenge. As parents, we are usually over-worked and under-rested, so we often find ourselves faced with these situations when cleaning up milk off the floor is the last thing we want to do.

Let's use some examples of alternatives:

- When your child wants to play ball in the house and knocks something over, instead of punishing or yelling, explain to him that this sort of activity is best played outside, then ask him to go outside and continue to play. You have now taught your child a valuable lesson of what is appropriate indoor and outdoor behavior.

- When your child wants to climb on the furniture, prop some pillows up with an old mattress instead, or encourage him to climb some rocks or go to the park and climb the play structures or trees instead.

- When your child wants to pull on the cat's tail, see if he wants to play tug-of-war with you instead.

- When your child starts mashing his food, give him some Play-Doh to play with instead.

The thing to remember is that if your children have an idea that you don't like, you don't need to reprimand them for it. Oftentimes their ideas come from a sincere desire to learn and explore the world. If you punish them for this, you will teach them to be less confident, less independent, and you will harm their natural sense of self-esteem. When you become upset with them, children feel bad about themselves and act out later. It becomes a vicious cycle.

By talking to them in a respectful and mature way, you will not only foster confidence and self-esteem, but you will also teach your children to talk to you in a respectful and mature way—because children model what you do, they will absorb this and use it.

Offering an alternative is an excellent way to treat your child with respect and, at the same time, it allows your child to be part of the decision-making process. If one alternative doesn't work for them, offer another. You can ask older children (over four) to offer their own alternatives.

This has happened countless times with my son. I offer him one thing and he says no; I get frustrated but keep my cool and offer him another. He eventually happily agrees. He's waiting for something that's closer to the experience he is exploring. For example, he's trying to hammer a nail he found outside into the floor; I offer him some wood, and he isn't interested. I then offer him Styrofoam, and he's excited and ready to work.

Try this the next time your child does something you don't want her to do:

First, evaluate the situation and think of an alternative. Refrain from getting upset at your child. Make it clear in your tone of voice (in a loving manner) that she needs to select an alternative because her present actions are not acceptable for you.

Asking a Question With Expression of Your Feelings

Do you remember the story about when our son was scratching the paint off the wall with a spoon? Instead of reacting, I applied the second, third, and fourth alternative to punishment. I evaluated the situation and asked him a question about what he was doing. He then told me he was taking snow off his spaceship.

Well, after he told me that, in order to get his cooperation I used another communication technique that helps children develop healthy empathy and respect. This is "expressing how you feel." By doing this you will teach your child how he is connected to the whole family's well-being, which will make him more considerate.

The next step is to express how you feel and offer an alternative.

For example:

"I don't want paint to come off the wall because then someone will have to repaint it, and I'm feeling a bit tired when I think about repainting. But I have a great idea of something we could do together that would be the same amount of fun..."

Did you notice how I expressed myself without applying any sense of blame or guilt onto the child for being responsible for my feelings? It is critical that you do not blame your child, or your child's actions, for your feelings.

The key is to communicate neutrally about your feelings.

For example:

Your child leaves her clothes on the floor. Instead of yelling, you can offer an explanation such as, "When you leave your clothes on the floor, I have to clean them up, and right now I feel a little tense about the possibility of picking them up, so could you please pick them up?"

In this example, you're actually making a request instead of offering an alternative. **Making a request** allows your child the opportunity to learn from finding her own suitable win-win alternative.

For example:

Your child is tracking muddy shoes into the house. Instead of yelling at your child or getting upset, you can simply reach out with your hand and physically stop her in a loving and gentle way, while also saying, *"Oh my! It looks like the floor is getting dirty. Let's take off your boots at the door so Mommy doesn't have to mop the floor again. Thanks, sweetie!"*

The real key is to ensure your child feels that you are not upset with her. Rather than reacting to what is happening, express how you feel and offer an alternative, or make a request that allows her the opportunity to solve the problem by finding her own alternative.

Do your best to keep the conversation neutral and avoid blame phrases. Distinguishing between blame and neutral communication can be a blurry line. It's best to keep in mind that your child wants nothing more than to feel connected with you.

What's a "Blame Phrase"?

The following are examples of blame phrases, each accompanied by an alternative.

Blame Phrase	"When you pinch me, it hurts me and makes me feel bad."
Neutral Phrase	"When you pinched my arm, it hurt because it startled me and hurt the skin on my arm."
Blame Phrase	"I'm so mad when you leave your clothes on the floor."
Neutral Phrase	"When you leave your clothes on the floor, it brings up strong emotions for me."
Blame Phrase	"You're a bad boy when you push your brother."
Neutral Phrase	"When your brother is pushed, he feels hurt, so that's why we don't push each other here. So please don't do that, sweetie."

Using neutral communication is a good way to demonstrate to your child how to express feelings intelligently instead of repressing them. Your child needs to know that feelings are OK and that he can express them appropriately. This way he will develop key emotional problem-solving skills that will be useful all his life.

Children do not need to take on the reactive emotions of adults, but often they do because of our lack of attention to their true needs. Offering a neutral explanation about how their behavior or actions are affecting you and your feelings is a form of respect and a form of education. It helps give your child more information about life by showing how his actions connect to you, the family, the home, the community, the environment, and the world.

Children need to feel safe to explore and learn about their world, through play and other activities. This is how they learn about themselves and how they belong as a part of the whole. By giving them the freedom and safety to explore their own potential in ways that benefit the whole family, you'll teach them how it can be more fun to cooperate and work with you instead of against you.

> "Whenever we admonish a child to 'be a good boy', we imply that we expect him to consider being bad and that we lack faith in his desire to be good."
>
> *- Rudolf Dreikurs*

What if you're really upset?

Usually, if you find yourself reacting strongly to something your child does or says, it is because your child is acting out and testing her limits. Many times our inability to practice non-reaction is because of other stresses in our life; we've had a long day, we're emotionally or physically exhausted, simply at the end of our rope, and so on. This usually stems from lack of support—this is where Adult-to-Adult Listening Time is critical for recharging our emotional batteries.

When you don't find yourself able to practice non-reaction, then just be authentic and express that emotion.

For example:

"Honey, Mommy is really upset right now. It's not your fault, and I'm not upset at you, but I'm feeling angry because of something else." Be authentic about your feelings instead of taking it out on your child or pretending everything is fine when you don't feel that way.

What if your child doesn't respond instantly?

Once you've expressed your feelings, offered an alternative, or made a request, you may not get the cooperation you're looking for. These techniques work very well when you have a strong connection with your child. Unfortunately, you are likely reading this book because your child is misbehaving now, and you may need some time to create a safe environment for him to respond positively to your alternatives.

We have practiced these techniques with our son since he was born. He's respected, listened to, cried with, and so on. In general, he is very cooperative and genuinely helpful, but he doesn't do EVERYTHING we ask—and we wouldn't want him to. Usually, children who are ultra-obedient are motivated by fear of punishment and consequently often develop low self-esteem and approval issues (which make them vulnerable to peer pressure later in life).

Parents who dominate their children through punishments, rewards, and threats raise children who have less capacity for creative problem solving because instead of learning how to think of ways to play and explore that are in harmony with the world around them, they are "forced" into doing things just because the authority "says so."

That's why there are so many peer pressure issues with teens and youth. Teens who have low self-esteem usually weren't allowed to safely and freely express and assert themselves while growing up. Instead, they were always told what to do and how to do it. Children who aren't allowed to say "no" to their parents will more likely succumb to peer pressure as teenagers and allow themselves to be dominated and manipulated as adults.

While children must be allowed to say "no" sometimes, there are certain rules that they simply must follow—and that's where you want to set a limit. Refer to the section about Setting Limits for more information on this.

Sometimes when you offer an alternative, your child won't want to do something else. Once you have explained that his behavior is not appropriate, he may simply stop and move on to something else, or he may throw a small tantrum and cry for a while. You will need to allow this and know that there is a deeper anxiety that needs to be resolved.

The key is in choosing your battles.

Avoid power struggles with your child, which will only set you up for defiance and rebellion as she gets older. It is much better to work WITH your child to help her see the benefit of a different course of action than to do something that causes you stress.

Above all, be sure to express through your communication—verbal, physical, and tone of voice—how much *you love them no matter what.* They need to know that they don't have to agree with you in order for you to love them.

Try this game. It's easy and works wonders.

Say silly things to your child mixed in with serious statements while telling him that your love for him is unconditional.

For example:

"I love you even if you eat a moldy apple."
"I love you even when you are angry."
"I love you even if you have a bath in the sprinkler."
"I love you even when you are sad."
"I love you even if you grow a tail and swing from the trees!"

This game is popular as it addresses important subjects but in a fun way and allows the child to relax any tension with "Natural Giggles."

Important Points:

- Establishing and maintaining a strong connection with your child is a key to reducing misbehavior. Your communication plays a significant role in establishing that connection. Communication includes what you say, as well as your body language and tone of voice.

- Be authentic with how you feel but never blame your child. Never use blame phrases; there is always an alternative.

- Focus on responding to your child instead of reacting out of your own anxiety. Remember that children are sponges and absorb what you do and say. Be the model of what you want. If you want your child to respect you and respond appropriately, then respect her and respond appropriately to her behavior.

- Young children never act out to hurt you, and older children rarely want to hurt you. They may want attention, or, much of the time they don't understand that their behavior has negative consequences. They don't see the world the same way you do.

- Saying "No!" (or equivalents such as "Stop!") may come across as harsh. Avoid it in non-emergencies and allow yourself to respond in a better, calmer way.

- Ensure your child knows you love them unconditionally, no matter what. Then act in accordance of that sentiment.

"Children seldom misquote you. In fact, they usually repeat word for word what you shouldn't have said."

- Author Unknown

CHAPTER 11

SETTING LIMITS

"Give me patience when little hands,
Tug at me with small demands,
Give me gentle words and smiling eyes
And keep my lips from sharp replies,
So in years to come when my house is still
Beautiful memories its rooms may fill."

- Stanley I. Greenspan

Limits are the borders between appropriate and inappropriate behavior, conduct, and action. The limits that exist in any family will define the culture and identity of the family. Consequently, the limits that a child grows up with form the very foundation of his identity.

Rules are also limits, as we can see how the rules of a game require all participants to abide by them in order for the game

to work properly. We encounter limits in our laws, our cultural moral codes, and our rules at school or work. We even find limits when it comes to nature and weather. For children, limits are the boundaries of what they know as reality.

Children are learning and growing in every moment in their play. They are incessantly constructing new knowledge based on how they choose to use their toys and manipulate the structures in their environment. They are continuously defining themselves and the world around them based on the limitations they meet and on how the children and adults around them respond.

> *"Setting limits gives your child something to define himself against. If you are able to set limits without being overly intrusive or controlling, you'll be providing him with a firm boundary against which he can test his own ideas."*
>
> *- Stanley I. Greenspan*

Why Children Test Limits

Einstein's statement, "We are limited only by our own imagination," contains one of the reasons why children will naturally and continuously test limits. We all know how big a child's imagination can be. They are born explorers; every moment for them is filled with learning and new knowledge.

We know that we make discoveries when we push limits. All the great inventions of our times have come about because someone challenged and tested the limits that we previously knew as reality. Just think of the invention of electricity, the telephone, air travel, and space travel. Hundreds of years before, we thought that the world was flat and that our limit was the end of the ocean.

In order for children to discover and learn, they need to feel secure in the limits that we provide for them. They need to push against the limits we give them so that they can feel as if they have a container in which they can grow.

It's healthy and good for children to test limits; it's their way of exploring their reality, developing their self-confidence, knowing their own limits, and gaining knowledge of their world. It's how they learn how to behave.

The key to successfully setting a limit is that it must be an *actual* limit; there should be no room for negotiating a limit, unless, of course, there is reasonable cause to be flexible with the limit. This is where the need to be objective and balanced between being firm and being flexible is important.

Generally, authoritarian parents are too firm, dominating, and rigid with limits, while permissive parents are too flexible, compromising, and disrespectful of limits themselves. With authoritarian discipline, the child will resent the limits and rebel against them if he deems them unreasonable or if they are not explained well. With permissive discipline, the child will easily trample over limits and chaos will reign.

With democratic discipline, however, the child learns to respect and appreciate limits because she doesn't feel like they are imposed on her. In democratic discipline, parents communicate the reason for the limit in a way that the child can understand based on her age.

Democratic discipline balances firmness and flexibility. There are many times when we must be firm, and children will often find the firmness a relief because, just like firm walls of a house, a firm limit becomes something they can depend on. However, we must always be aware that sometimes being more flexible with our limits is quite appropriate. The reason for this is that as children grow, so do their limits; and while we may limit a toddler from using a sharp knife to keep her safe, there comes a time when it's appropriate for a mature enough child to learn how to handle a sharp blade carefully.

Here is an example of balancing firmness and flexibility in setting a simple limit. A friend gave us a nice couch, but it was white, and it would get dirty quite quickly with kids around, so we needed to get it covered. Before we covered it, I wanted to prevent it from getting too dirty, so I told my son that under no circumstances could he put his feet on the couch because it would get dirty. He responded by asking if he could go on it with his feet if he first washed them in the bathtub. I told him that was a good idea, but his feet would still likely pick up some dirt between the bathroom and couch, so I reaffirmed the limit and told him that wouldn't work.

He then responded by asking me if he washed his feet, then wore socks between the bathtub and the couch, could he then take off his socks and put his clean feet on the couch. Well, that's a good question, I thought, and I realized that in this case the couch would not be at risk of getting dirty. This was the time to be flexible with the limit, and I told him that it would be fine. If I had still maintained the limit even though the couch would not get dirty, I would have lost my son's respect because children are very quick to see if a limit or rule is simply dogmatic or if it is reasonable.

By being flexible in this case, I not only won my son's respect, he also gained more self-confidence in creative problem solving. In addition, it reaffirmed my willingness to listen, cooperate, and be flexible so that we can all get along in the best way possible. Because children follow our example, my son in turn became more willing to listen, cooperate, and be flexible as well.

Saying "No"

If you have a hard time saying "no" to your child, sticking with your "no," feeling guilty for saying "no," or letting your child negotiate or manipulate his way around your "no," then you probably use permissive discipline. If you can say "no" easily and stick with your "no" just as easily, then you probably tend towards a more authoritarian discipline. Permissive parents eventually run out of patience and swing to authoritarian discipline with a harsh and loud "no!"

Sometimes saying "no" is hard because of *how* we say it. When young children are allowed the opportunity to really play and enjoy the zest of childhood, they can feel quite hurt, isolated, and criticized by the slightest harshness. When we say "no," we are essentially setting a limit. If a child who's already had enough sugar wants a second serving of cake, you are setting a healthy limit by saying "no." Yet if you say "no" without kindness, respect, and consideration, your child may feel quite disconnected by your response. In addition, she will end up saying "no" to you without kindness, respect and consideration—because children always model our example.

We want to encourage children to enjoy free spontaneous play because they are learning in every moment of their play. But there are times when their experiment may not be working, their play becomes unsafe, or they begin to exhibit unkind behavior towards others. To help our children continue experimenting, exploring, playing, and learning, we must step in with a limit and redirect them towards a safer and more harmonious direction.

As a parent, you are naturally inclined to say "no" when your child is approaching something dangerous. In emergencies, saying "no!" forcefully may be imperative. As we learned in the previous chapter, yelling "no" forcefully, with our voice filled with tension and concern will likely freeze the child on the spot and protect her from the danger. Saying "no!" can save your child's life in some situations.

It's when we begin to say "no" in other situations with a harsh tone that a child can become discouraged. When you use the word "no" repeatedly with a child of any age, the child can become so discouraged that it may even threaten her self-esteem and autonomy.

Saying "no" with the tones of harshness, anger, frustration, disapproval, criticism, or impatience can cause such a rift in your connection with your children that it can stop their thinking process and cause a lot of confusion and hurts. Just as they may physically freeze on the spot when you belt out a loud "no!" to protect them from danger, a harsh "no!" causes them to freeze in non-dangerous situations. If you shout out "no!" when your children make a mistake or begin to do something they shouldn't, they will likely "shut down" emotionally as they attempt to cope with the feelings that arise from your yell.

When children are going off-track, the last thing we want to do is to shut down their thinking and disconnect with them because they won't learn anything in this state. If you yell at them for running across the street without looking, they will be more likely to repeat this mistake because the emotions that came up from being yelled at will be clouding their ability to really take in what you're saying. A far better approach is to gently capture their full attention, then kindly, clearly, and respectfully explain to them the importance of looking both ways across the street.

This is why yelling and punishing are not effective ways to teach children. Instead of instilling them with the wisdom and knowledge we want them to remember, punishment and harshness fill them with more tension and stress, which further impedes their thinking process.

Children who hear "no" all the time may begin to second-guess their judgment and ability. This can manifest as all kinds of confidence and esteem issues. If your child appears shy, timid, withdrawn, or needy, become aware of how you set verbal limits with him. Are you saying "no" frequently? Is your tone of voice encouraging or critical? Note your tone of voice, body language, and the words you use to set the limit. Do you give him an age-appropriate explanation without emotion or criticism?

By responding proactively without anger, without frustration, and without anxiety, we can teach our children more effectively than by reacting harshly and impulsively. When we stay calm, our child stays calm. When we slow down, our child slows down. When we set verbal limits with our child, it's best to save "no!" for when we really need it.

If you say "no" frequently during your child's play, such as, *"No, don't climb on that structure!"* or *"No, don't run around the house!"* or *"No, stop, don't play with that!"* he will soon become immune to "no." Defiance and rebellion will become the normal state of being as the child no longer has any respect for "no." If you say "no" all the time, your child will soon begin to ignore you.

So what are your options?

As we discussed in the *Connective Communication* section, there are some ways to redirect your child without saying "no," such as:

"Not right now, sweetie."
"That's a good idea, however right now we're going to _____ because _____."
"I'm afraid not, darling."
"Not today, dear."
"Unfortunately not, my sweetheart."

These are all effective ways to say "no" without discouraging your child. Remember, it's the way you say it that matters. The statements above are difficult to say harshly, but they remain negative. Can you think of any more ways to say "no"?

Setting Verbal Limits

As we discussed in *Connective Communication*, if your child spills a glass of water when getting up from the dining table and you react by yelling ***OH NO!!!!! WHAT HAVE YOU DONE?!! PAY MORE ATTENTION! YOU'RE ALWAYS MAKING A MESS!*** Then your child will freeze in fear and not be quite sure what happened or what to do next.

The only recourse for children in this situation is to feel bad, and they will begin to feel less confident because they will begin to believe that they always "make a mess." You are basically programming them to be clumsy! Also, they'll be less likely to help with chores or clean up because they will believe that they're incapable of being tidy and they will undoubtedly upset their parents again by making another mess.

If we take this same situation and use a democratic response, we could respond with something like, *"Whoops! Well, I guess we'll have to clean that up."* Using proactive and inclusive language with a big smile to show encouraging body language, the child will typically respond by immediately and joyfully cleaning it up. If they are too young to do it themselves, then they'll be enthusiastically helpful. By keeping the response light and proactive, we maintain our clear thinking state by keeping heavy or intense emotions out of our reaction.

The result is that we do not pass undue pressure, tension, or stress onto our kids when they make mistakes. By remaining tension-free, your children will remember the incident better and become more conscious and careful the next time they get up from the table.

Accidents and mistakes simply happen in life. As we get older, we continue to make mistakes. If we learn from our mistakes and avoid repeating them, then we become wise. Punishments, threats, and stress do not help us avoid mistakes. On the contrary, we learn best when we are in a relaxed, receptive and happy state of mind.

When your child makes a mistake, take a moment before you react and think about the best response to meet his needs. You may choose to provide a simple explanation that allows your child to see how he can adjust his actions. This can help shift your child's attention back to the present moment, helping him be more aware, careful, and attentive to his environment.

Democratic discipline teaches through Natural Consequences, which help develop creative problem-solving skills with an optimistic and inclusive sense of responsibility. The way to build

this buoyant sense of responsibility is through maintaining a close connection while teaching your child the proactive way to handle mistakes. This teaches your child not to stress out over little things, which helps eliminate unnecessary obstacles for greater success in life.

By using "we" language in your verbal limits, you'll engender a team mentality to dealing with problems and help your child be more focused on the needs of the situation rather than only his own needs, which we call being "situation-centered."

Children thrive with limits when they're set kindly. Verbal limits not only help restore order and keep balance in the home, but they also create an open dialogue for you and your child. This is very important because as your child ages, he will often be able to process his experiences more easily with you through dialogue if you have a strong connection with him. However, if your child doesn't respond to verbal limits, then you may need to consider setting a Healing Limit to return your child to a sense of connection, good judgment, and clear thinking.

Using Limits to Create a Healing Space

If a child is acting out-of-control, aggressively, reactively, or overly emotionally, she may have an accumulation of stress that needs to heal. Behind stress is always a sense of disconnection. Perhaps she feels disconnected from her parents, other children, or her overall environment. Remember that a child's connection to her parent is her link to survival. It is her instinctual drive to react emotionally by crying or acting out when she senses her connection to her parents is threatened. We often see that the younger they are, the more they seem to act from their instinctive drives than from their logical reasoning.

Babies who always cry desperately when their mother puts them down are displaying this instinctive drive. Babies and children who are clingy and desperate to stay close to their mothers and parents are simply expressing that their need for security and safety is not met. The reason why some babies won't give their mother a moment's rest is that their sense of connection is often somehow broken, which means the mother needs to reevaluate how she's bonding with her child.

The **Attachment Theory** provides a good example for emotionally reassuring the bond with a baby and child. **Attachment Parenting** follows the examples of less technology-driven cultures where babies are carried on the backs of their mothers everywhere for the first months.

Most mothers give so much of their time to their babies: playing with them, entertaining them, feeding them, bathing them, changing them, etc. One can easily wonder how such a pampered baby can feel disconnected with so much love and attention. If we remember that a baby's sense of connection is very fragile and that it can be easily broken through feelings of isolation, criticism, over-stimulation, or physical hurts, then we soon see how many small incidents can be quite stressful for them.

Furthermore, if a baby is hushed, rocked, or prevented from crying, the baby never gets to work out the associated feelings of disconnection. These repressed feelings keep the sense of disconnection intact. Even when the baby is safe and fully cared for he may act anxious, fearful, and desperately needy. His strong feelings of disconnection are the cause for this fear and desperation. To release it, his sense of disconnection needs to heal. The tears must be allowed to flow freely and for as long as necessary.

Setting a Healing Limit allows your child to release the unresolved tension, stress, and hurts by creating an emotional safety cocoon. Creating an emotional safety cocoon is based on the idea that children—and adults—heal best within a safe container of loving attention and support. Unbending limits of unconditional love are the walls of this container.

One thing to remember is that it's quite common for some children to avoid expressing these deep feelings, especially if repression of feelings or tears was previously encouraged in their home. Boys tend to avoid their feelings more than girls due to the old autocratic social and cultural standard of "boys don't cry." However, when we examine the health, psychological, and physiological benefits of crying, we can see how beneficial it is for boys to cry when they need to. Even we, as adults, benefit greatly from having a good cry.

Other children have no problem crying. Some are just brimming on the edge of a tantrum, waiting for a chance to let it all out. That's why we don't consider tantrums to be "bad" behavior; on the contrary, they are a healing reaction. Tantrums and other challenging behaviors are simply your child's way of saying: *"Okay, I'm having some intense feelings now—can you give me a hand?"* This is exactly when it's the right time to set a Healing Limit.

4 STAGES OF SETTING A HEALING LIMIT

1 If the child is at risk of hurting himself or someone else, then first you must ensure everyone's safety. Start by physically limiting the child by gently blocking him with your hand, arm, or body. There are also times when you may simply be able to use a verbal limit to protect a child from harm.

2 Focus your loving attention on connecting with the child. Depending on where the child is, you may be able to make physical contact with him by putting a hand on his shoulder, back, arm, or hand. The goal is to establish eye contact with your child. Through that eye contact, communicate how much you love him. If the child resists, avoids, and runs from your loving eye contact and physical touch, then this is a sign to give him a little more space, without reducing the loving attention. Just give your child a little more physical and emotional distance while maintaining your stance of reaching for him. Keep looking to connect through your eye contact. As your child begins to relax into your attention, his sense of connection will solidify. Then he will move closer and closer to you, perhaps eventually into your arms staring into your loving eyes.

3 Listen to the strong feelings that come up as the tensions drain. Continue to affirm your child's connection through your words and gestures until she stops crying on her own. Let the feelings drain to completion, but don't let her feel alone while she is releasing them. Do not rush her to composure. Refrain from using terms like "there, there" or "it will be ok." Also, try not to "pat on the back" as this is a very uncomfortable sensation and not conducive to establishing and maintaining a connection. Hold firmly and gently.

4 Repeat the limit every time the behavior arises again. Consistency is important to make a permanent change in their behavior. Consistently limiting difficult behavior shows your child that he is welcome to express it in more healthy ways like crying, talking, and connecting with you, but unpleasant behavior will be lovingly limited immediately.

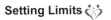

While you do this, it's crucial to remain physically close and emotionally available and attentive to your child. There may be strong feelings or hurts that are underneath his behavior, so he may try to avoid connecting with you. That's quite natural; just keep reaching through his disconnection with your eye contact, physical closeness, body posture, tone of voice, and your supportive words.

Be prepared for anger and rage to spill out. These strong emotions often cover up fear and terror from unresolved past hurts that need to heal. If your child begins to rage, tantrum, or cry, then the healing is happening. Your child may try to hit you or strike out physically. If she does, gently stop her. Your role now is to stay loving, connected, listening, and non-reactive, while keeping everyone safe.

Tantrums usually come about when a child can't get a control pattern, comfort object, or desperate desire fulfilled. Parents who always give in to these desires to avoid or to stop tantrums will soon find themselves exhausted and resentful with a child who is disrespectful and ungrateful.

While your child is working through these feelings, don't expect her to be in a thinking state. Don't try to pull her into a thinking state by asking her questions or trying to soothe her through intellectual rationale. Children may sometimes rage and say the worst possible things about you, others, or themselves. They may try to avoid releasing their feelings by distracting you or by trying to trigger or fight with you, anything to stop the emotions as they begin expressing them. If this happens, just ignore the terrible things they say and keep reaching through their disconnection through your eye contact, body language, and direct warm communication.

Here is something to keep in mind—the more they say things like "I hate you," the more desperate they are for a real connection with you.

Often, while we attempt to redirect our children away from their behaviors that are quite challenging, these behaviors persist despite our best efforts. When this happens, it's a good indicator that we may not be addressing the correct reason for their behavior. When we can attribute their behavior to stress, unresolved hurts, and accumulated tension, then it's a good time to set a Healing Limit. Just remember: Every tear heals.

Control patterns

A control pattern is anything used externally to repress or distract your child from expressing his feelings. They are coping mechanisms often developed as an attachment to comfort objects or obsessive habits. Control patterns are used to cope with accumulated tension or hurts because they allow the child to feel a sense of control and power when he feels powerless. They are easy to recognize when a child desperately clings to the particular pattern.

Examples of comfort objects are blankets, favorite toys, clothes, soothers, or bottles for younger children. Examples of coping habits are sugary sweets, treats, certain foods, TV, video games, habitual web browsing, over-eating, or nail biting. With toddlers and babies, we also see such coping habits as comfort nursing, thumb sucking, rocking, or carrying.

Control patterns are addictive in nature and may manifest in adolescence or adulthood in addictive tendencies such as food addictions, drinking, drugs, smoking, sexual addictions, affairs, and gambling. They can also manifest in adults as less offensive

patterns and habits such as nail biting, caffeine addiction, binge eating, shopping addiction, regular arguments with other adults, and overworking or staying too busy.

Control patterns "soothe" temporarily, but they don't have a lasting effect because they don't heal the hurts underneath the desperation. Until this desperation is faced and the underlying hurts are given the chance to come out, the child will continue to need more and more soothing, especially when encountering other stressful circumstances in life. As such, they will get into the habit of turning to control patterns instead of healing from their pain. We see that adults who smoke cigarettes after stressful situations exhibit this same behavior.

Control patterns cause children to disassociate from their pain, which leads to numbness and poor attention. Moreover, because control patterns allow children to cling to an object or pattern, they cause them to be insensitive to people and their environment.

Have you ever noticed how toddlers or children who suck their thumbs are often in a "trance-like" state? Their eyes will often glaze over, and they become less responsive. They will also appear somewhat closed off from the world around them.

If you use toys, pacifiers, or rocking to stop a baby's tears, then you will be teaching her to disassociate from her own feelings, setting the foundations of dissociative patterns that may develop later. When children are not allowed to express emotions in front of others, they feel isolated and insecure in their pain. Control patterns become a replacement for an open, loving, and clear connection with their parents—a barrier between themselves and their parents.

Luckily, control patterns are easily broken through a Healing Limit. The first step is to become *aware* of your child's control pattern.

Does your child have one or more control patterns? Write them down here:

_____

_____

_____

_____

_____

_____

Through time, or through healing, some control patterns will vanish forever and new ones may appear. Whenever a child isn't able to process a stressful experience or has an unmet need, she may begin to develop a pattern to cope with the situation, particularly when the stress is repeated or is a consistent part of her day (for example: an ongoing divorce, illness in the family, bully at school, etc.). Seeing violence daily in the media, busy days, or pressure from tests at school can all be sources of ongoing stress for kids, which can lead to the development of control patterns.

Ready to limit control patterns?

Here are a few tips for you. We recommend you follow this basic framework to begin to learn how to set a kind limit.

We suggest planning a time when you know you can focus your attention and your reservoir of patience is full. Be prepared to listen to your child's deeper feelings for forty-five minutes or more to help completely dissolve the sense of desperation that may come up when facing the control pattern. Interrupting control patterns with limits will often bring up a tantrum, strong crying or even raging.

Don't expect the control pattern to be gone after simply one healing session as your child may likely still have more feelings inside. This control pattern may be months or years old, so it may take some repeated limits to undo it. You may limit the control pattern once or even twice and find that your child will still go back to it. If your child does, keep setting the limit. You can try saying something like:

"I love you, sweetie, AND I think it's best if you don't use your soother anymore. I am going to stay close and listen."

Every time your child asks for his comfort object, you can just repeat the same thing: *"Sweetie, I love you, and I want to be close to you. In being close to you, I don't think you need your soother right now."* You may even find that after your child has released the desperation around the control pattern, she may still test the limit out of curiosity. This is a good sign of the improvement she is making in becoming stress-free.

Limiting Soothers and Pacifiers

If your baby or toddler has a pacifier or soother, the first step in helping him overcome his control patterns is to limit it. Comfort items that have no beneficial side effects include soothers and pacifiers, candies, video game players, cable TV, and similar distractions. These you can simply throw away so that they are no longer available. The value of distraction that these control patterns bring you can sometimes feel worth it, particularly if you have a stressful life. It can feel easier to give your baby a soother over listening to your baby cry through some tension.

In our opinion, soothers only encourage control patterns and oral fixations and don't do children any good. There is the argument that they are good for babies to chew on while they're teething. However, there are better options to help teething. If your child is having a hard time while teething, there are three things to consider before giving him a soother to chew on. Please be very careful with choking hazards.

First, realize that the emotional effect of soothers leads to control patterns, which we've just discussed. Secondly, research nutritional advice for teething; sometimes changes in your child's diet or your diet (if you're breast-feeding) can really help teething issues. Finally, be aware that although most soothers on the market are made of safe material, there are still some that are not. Give your child natural and safe items to chew on, such as licorice root or cinnamon sticks instead of plastic or rubber.

Limiting Frustration and Whining

Your six-year-old girl knows how to tie her shoes, but on this occasion she can't seem to get it quite right. She begins to get frustrated. You are standing by, observing and allowing her the space to figure it out for herself. She starts getting very upset because she is having a hard time tying her shoes and speaks to you in a whiny voice, saying:

"I want YOU to tie my shoes! WAAAAAAAAAAAAH, I want YOU to DO IT, Mommy!"

Because you know that she already knows how to tie her shoes, you can discern that the reason for her behavior is not her lack of ability. You know she's properly nourished and rested, so you can assume that she doesn't need food and isn't tired. And you remember that she's been acting tense since she returned from school the day before. So, in this situation, you would discern that the reason for her behavior is that she's tense about something that happened at her school.

The issue is actually not "what" happened, but the residual tension and stress that is carrying over into her actions and attention. She likely just had an experience that she's having a hard time processing. Perhaps it is quite serious and needs your intervention, or perhaps it's not a big deal at all, just a story another child told her. The only way you're going to find out what's really bothering her is to help her by facing the current issue (in this example, tying her shoe).

If you turn the emotional interaction into an intellectual one and say, "What's the matter with you, did something happen at school?" you'll only make her feel more isolated and confused as you bring her attention farther away from the present moment. Also, your assessment that something happened at school could be wrong, so your intellectual probing may just confuse your child more.

The key therefore is to set a limit that will bring her into the present moment so that she can face the challenge that's right in front of her. If your child needs to release some tension, she will let you know through her response.

An appropriate limit in this situation would be to start with a verbal limit, indicating encouragingly to her that you believe in her ability to figure out how to tie her shoes. In a loving, patient, and caring tone, you could say, *"Sweetie, I think I will let you do it your way."*

By using the verbal limit to turn her attention back on her own stumbling block, you give her a chance to increase her confidence, autonomy, self-understanding, and, most importantly, you allow her to really face her emotional and mental state head-on. If she does not have a lot of tension but is just preoccupied with something in her mind and not paying attention, this response alone may be enough for her to "snap out of it" and be able to tie her shoes without any more issues.

If she does have tension and stress, her reaction will quickly let you know. She may start whining, throwing a tantrum, yelling, crying, and even attacking someone. This shows you that she needs a Healing Limit. If, on the other hand, you succumb to her whining and tie her shoes for her, the underlying tension will continue to linger, impede her thinking, and resurface in unpleasant behavior.

If you're on the way out the door and late for something, and it's not a good time to set a Healing Limit, then you may opt to tie them for her and try to help her heal later. If you do have the time, it's worth setting a limit to face the frustration and whining head on. That way you can resolve it immediately instead of having to deal with her whining all day long.

When setting a Healing Limit, allow the tears to flow. Don't rush your child to composure. Thirty minutes, one hour, or sometimes even more time may be needed for a child to release all the pent-up tension. If she erupts into an immediate tantrum, then you know that she has a need to express and expel some stress. After her feelings are out, she will likely go back to her warm, giggly, and clear-thinking self.

If your child's whining or frustration always comes during particular daily activities, then you can plan ahead and start setting the limit early.

Limiting Temper Tantrums

The first thing we need to realize about tantrums is that they are not bad. Tantrums are a child's way of saying, *"I'm having a really hard time dealing with some strong feelings. Can you please help me?"* Tantrums usually indicate that a child could benefit from a Healing Limit.

The key to ending tantrums is to let them flow to completion. Tantrums are like fire. Strong feelings are the fuel for tantrums. If you let the fire (tantrums) burn out all the fuel (tension), then soon the fuel will be all burnt out and the fire will disappear. That's exactly how tantrums act—as a channel to relieve all the built-up pressure and stress. The listening and full attention you provide during a Healing Limit act as the air that the fire needs in order to burn easily and securely.

As we stated earlier in the chapter, tantrums usually come about when a child can't get a control pattern, comfort object, or desperate desire fulfilled. Parents who always give in to these desires to avoid or to stop tantrums will soon find themselves exhausted and resentful with a child who is disrespectful and ungrateful.

Here is a summary of the four stages mentioned previously for limiting a temper tantrum:	
First stage	If the child is at risk of hurting himself or another, then first you must ensure everyone's safety.
Second stage	Focus your loving attention on connecting with the child.
Third stage	Listen to the strong feelings that come up as the tensions drain.
Fourth stage	Repeat the limit every time the behavior arises again.

Choose a good time to set limits with tantrums. Sometimes they will come up unexpectedly somewhere quite inconvenient, so you may choose to wait until another time. If you choose to wait, then you can redirect their attention away from the tantrum, even giving in to their object of desire simply to win some cooperation. Although it's a short-term solution, rewards can be convenient in such cases.

If your child already throws tantrums, then you will likely know some key triggers for your child and you can actually prepare to set a limit beforehand. Be sure that you set these limits when your attention and patience are topped up. You will need to give your child plenty of positive energy while you listen to strong feelings.

If you give in to their object of desire or control pattern at any point, you will stop the tantrum and consequently stop the

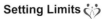

healing. You can, of course, do this if you choose; just be aware that unless the tantrum is given air to burn through all the fuel of feelings, then the fire will likely blaze up again.

Limiting Aggression and Violence

You should not allow your children to hurt you, themselves or anyone else, nor allow them to break anything while you create a Healing Limit. If your child does try to hit, bite, kick, or attack you, someone else, or even tries to hurt himself, set a loving verbal limit as well as a protective physical one. You can simply say, *"Sweetheart, I'm not going to let you hurt me,"* while physically stopping him from hitting you or anyone else. The majority of parents in this situation would get angry with their child and punish him, yelling, "Go to your room!" By this point in the book you've already guessed that reacting in this way will give you the opposite result that you want.

So do not punish them because this will make them feel even more isolated. The sooner you can make them feel connected again, the sooner their tension will be healed and they'll return to a state of loving and aware interaction. When children exhibit violent or aggressive behaviors, they usually desperately need a Healing Limit. It is important to remember that children really just want to feel connected, so their violence will dissolve as soon as they have a chance to drain their feelings of isolation, hurts, or confusion.

Violence and aggression are outward attacks against limits of acceptable and safe behavior. By understanding this, you can ignore the fact that they're using their words and body to do and say hurtful things. They may say they hate you and the most awful things, but understand that this is just their way of reaching out for emotional assistance.

159

As an adult, you are surely agile and strong enough to stop a child from hurting someone when having a raging tantrum. Don't respond to the content of the raging, just remain present and remind yourself that all this rage needs to come out for him to heal the hurts hidden deep down inside. Keep connecting with his heart and ignore all the ugly displays of his rage.

Remember, if you must physically restrain your child, make sure you avoid heavy or hard physical restraint. You should try to relax your muscles and feel as if you are very soft and receptive. If he triggers you and you become upset, then you must be extra careful and use as little physical restraint as possible until you can cool yourself down. When your child displays aggression or violence, it's important for you to let go of your own personal issues and focus on being present with your child.

When considering setting limits, remember that there is no single right way to respond to your child's behavior. Every response should be based on your assessment of your child's needs. If he needs to reconnect and heal from some hurts, then a Healing Limit would be appropriate. If he has another unmet need, then you may need to set a limit in order to meet that need of his.

After you assess his needs, you may feel that setting a limit isn't necessary at all. Maybe it would be as simple as setting up some Self-Directed Play time or some Play Attention Time for him to meet his needs and resolve the behavior. First, be clear on the need, then respond based on that.

"Our children are counting on us to provide two things: consistency and structure. Children need parents who say what they mean, mean what they say, and do what they say they are going to do."

- Barbara Coloroso

CHAPTER 12

ADULT-TO-ADULT LISTENING TIME

"Listening is a magnetic and strange thing, a creative force. The friends who listen to us are the ones we move toward. When we are listened to, it creates us, makes us unfold and expand."

- Karl A. Menninger

We are asking a lot of you. You need to be infinitely patient. You need to set your own feelings and reactions aside so you can respond positively to your children, even when they are causing disasters around you.

To get to where you want to be, you are going to need to recharge your own emotional batteries from time to time. We understand that sometimes there's very little time to do this, but it's critical.

It's like when the flight attendants do the safety announcement on an airplane; they explain that if the oxygen masks fall, you should secure your own before putting one on your child. The point is that you need to fill your own "emotional reserves" in order to give more to your child.

Regular emotional support for yourself with another adult will fill up your emotional reserves by helping you drain your own tension, stress, and pressure. When you are tension-free, your patience is multiplied.

Remember, children are sponges and mirrors. If you are stressed, they will be. If you are angry, they will be upset. Taking care of yourself is critical to taking care of your child.

Being listened to, uninterrupted, with the full attention of a supportive friend, enables us to spill out the myriad of emotional feelings that we otherwise bottle up. These repressed emotions accumulate, build stress and affect our natural zest for life and good judgment. These accumulated tensions cause havoc in our personal relationships and negatively affect our sense of connection with those we love. When parents are stressed, it becomes difficult to meet our child's needs for full attention, and nearly impossible to listen patiently to our child's strong feelings.

Adult-to-Adult Listening Time is when another adult listens to you with his or her full attention, without judgment, advice, or even feedback. It's scheduled time where you can simply let all your thoughts, worries, emotions, stress, and feelings come out in the presence of another's loving attention. This method is modeled after "co-counseling" or "re-evaluation counseling."

Most people have had few opportunities to enjoy such support throughout their lives. This chapter will outline how you can integrate this life-changing routine into your own life and reap the many benefits that come with it. Having more patience and fewer triggers, feeling more love and less stress, and thinking clearer, while reacting less impulsively, are just the most obvious rewards that come from practicing regular Adult-to-Adult Listening Time.

You can do this with your spouse, a family member, or a friend. If it is possible in your schedule, we recommend being listened to a few times a week for twenty minutes or more.

Sometimes as busy parents, we can fall into feeling isolated. Depending on where you live and on your own situation, you may even think that there is no one who would be willing or able to schedule this with you. We understand how it may feel difficult to reach out for support when you feel isolated.

If you find yourself facing doubts, fears, or challenges about reaching out to someone to engage in this activity with you, we encourage you to follow the Nike adage of "just do it!" Besides, your doubts and fears are mostly unfounded. Friends love to help friends—if a friend asked you to listen, wouldn't you? Of course you would, and you'd probably feel honored if they asked YOU.

> *"It's not only children who grow. Parents do too. As much as we watch to see what our children do with their lives, they are watching us to see what we do with ours. I can't tell my children to reach for the sun. All I can do is reach for it, myself."*
>
> *- Joyce Maynard*

Finding a Listening Partner

First, think of a friend or an acquaintance who you think has good listening skills. Invite this person to meet with you at a scheduled time to exchange listening time. You will need to train your friend; let him or her know that you will exchange equal time, so that each person has a chance to be listened to.

If you can't think of anyone, then the first step is to reach out within your community to find someone. Consider parents at your child's school or playgroups, or perhaps you may use online services or attend local events where you may meet some new people who could fill this role for you. You can also conduct an online search for "co-counseling" or "re-evaluation counseling" to see if there's a group in your area. You may be able to find someone in that group with whom you can share listening time.

Beginning Listening Time

Once you have found a friend to practice this with you, you can begin the sharing and listening time. We will refer to the listener as the "counselor" and the person being listened to as the "client." The time period devoted to the listening and sharing will be called a "session." We recommend starting out with twenty-minute sessions.

The client will talk and share emotions, tears, and laughter for a twenty-minute session, while the counselor listens without interrupting or giving advice. The counselor will focus on being warm, deeply caring, and attentive.

The counselor does NOT give advice, offer a solution, or help with any issue. He or she is only there to listen empathetically.

165

Emotional Healing Time

When you are in the client role, this is your time to work on any emotional issues that may be bubbling on the surface. You can also explore other issues and unresolved hurts from the past. You may share your personal history, including your history with your child, or even your own childhood.

If tears come, stay with these feelings, as the tears will drain the emotional burdens. Similarly, stay with any thoughts that stir laughter. Return to that thought or memory that allows the gales of laughter to burst forth, healing many tensions. These feelings may come out instantly as soon as your friend begins giving you full, loving attention. Or, you may find that you need to talk until the deeper feelings rise to the surface.

Closing the Session

The counselor should inform the client when there are five minutes remaining. The counselor should use these final five minutes to pull the client's attention back to the present. You can do this by noticing items you enjoy in your present environment. You can take note of the colors, shapes, and objects that surround you.

The counselor can help pull the client's attention back to the present, which is particularly helpful when the client has been working through many strong feelings. The counselor can do this by asking the client questions like, "Tell me all the things you see that are green," or "Tell me all the things that you see that are round or circular," or "If you could make a sculpture with three random objects in this room, which would you use, and how would you put them together?"

You can also pull your attention back to the present by thinking about something that you are looking forward to in the day or weeks ahead. They could be simple things, like a flower garden you will see on your daily walk, your planned visit to see a best friend, an upcoming trip or holiday, playing with your child, etc.

This may seem silly at first, but it works. Bringing your awareness back to the present is **vital to transition** out of being a client and being attentive enough to navigate back into the flow of your upcoming schedule.

An Equal Exchange

After one person finishes being the client for twenty minutes, you begin another session reversing the roles: the previous counselor will be the client, and the previous client will provide he or she full, loving attention as the counselor. This process allows equal time between you and your listening partner because we all need and deserve such listening time. Additionally, this keeps the relationship equal.

Schedule Listening Time into Your Weekly Routine

Schedule these regular sessions into your weekly routine with your listening partner. As you continue to do these sessions, you'll find that your attention and peace of mind will continue to increase. You'll find yourself much less reactive and more present to your child's needs.

Listening Phone Support

Once you have become familiar with using Adult-to-Adult Listening Time, you and your listening partner can also exchange "Listening Phone Support." This is structured in the same manner of exchanging listening time, except it's done on the phone. This can be very beneficial and convenient.

Please ensure you are fully present for these calls. Do not multitask and avoid places or situations that could cause you distraction. This is true for both counselor and client roles.

Should You Cry in Front of Your Child?

There will be times when you are with your child and feeling so stressed that you can tell that a good cry would help you regain composure and drain the tension. Your listening partner may not be available for immediate support, so why not just let the tears come out?

Modern society is quite primitive in their view of crying and tears. It's still seen in many cultures as a sign of weakness, when, in fact, it's a perfectly effective biological healing mechanism. Crying is natural, for kids and for adults. Some people think that it's not correct to cry in front of your child, but if tears and crying is understood from the basis of healing, then there are even benefits to crying in front of your child.

You should never attempt to use your child as a counselor. The Adult-to-adult Listening model should only be used with adults, not children. The most important consideration when you feel the urge to cry around your children is their needs and their state. If your children's needs are satisfied, then you will likely have plenty of freedom to have a good cry in front of them.

If your child is tense himself, or if you discern that it may be better for you to cry in another room instead of in front of your child, you can do this by simply communicating with your child. Tell him that you're going in the other room to cry *"to get my sad feelings out."* If your child is feeling tense, he may not want you to leave his side, so, in this case, it will be better to just let some tears come out in front of him.

Be very aware when you cry in front of your child that you do not lose the connection with her. Do not get lost in the feelings and fall into an indulgence of self-pity and depression. If you have a hard time being present again after having a cry, practice the methods recommended previously that are used to close the Adult-to-Adult Listening Time. Pull your attention back to the present by noticing objects in your environment and of thinking of things you're looking forward to.

When you maintain a loving connection with your children and don't blame them for your frustrations, crying in front of them often makes them instantly more considerate, compassionate, and sensitive to your needs as well. When it's understood in your family culture that crying is used to relieve tension and stress, your whole family may develop a very loving and supportive attitude as you all learn to help meet each other's needs.

Important Points:

- Do an online search for "co-counseling" or "re-evaluation counseling" to see if there's a group in your area. You may be able to find someone in that group to share listening time with you.

- The purpose of this time is for you to be listened to so that you can expel your emotions and stress.

- Make sure that as the "counselor" you are only listening and **not** offering advice or asking questions. It's critical to **listen only**.

169

- If you need to have a good cry but can't set up some Adult-to-Adult Listening Time, or if you need to expel the feelings right away, then make sure your child's needs are completely tended to and have a good cry by yourself.

CHAPTER 13

FAMILY MEETINGS

> *"If you want to build a ship, don't drum up people to collect wood and don't assign them tasks and work, but rather teach them to long for the endless immensity of the sea."*
>
> *- Antoine de Saint-Exupery*

amily meetings are a great way to build the foundation for cooperative and happy children. The benefits of having regular family meetings are many.

Firstly, they meet your child's needs for feeling a sense of belonging and participation in the family. Secondly, they meet your child's need for attention, information, and autonomy. Finally, family meetings act as a space where you and your child can really both listen to and hear each other. Without this level of communication, cooperation is impossible without coercion and authoritarianism.

Family Meetings are approached in the spirit of loving appreciation and optimistic problem solving. They act as a space where all family members build the habit of teamwork while sharing their thoughts, feelings, and love with each other. Family meetings become the forum where announcements about future plans, changes in routines, and schedules are shared.

This creates a great nurturing environment where your children can have so many of their needs met at once. This is a time for your children to feel engaged and included in the plans and decisions because they are communicated with and treated as equals. This has the effect of making them cooperative when carrying through on any new changes or agreements. Family meetings are particularly effective with older children and teenagers.

> *"You don't really understand human nature unless you know why a child on a merry-go-round will wave at his parents every time around - and why his parents will always wave back."*
>
> *- William D. Tammeus*

The Intention is Connection

The intention of family meetings is primarily to build connection. Introducing ideas, negotiating chores, bringing up issues, or any other agendas are important. However, the number one priority is to connect with your child and for her to feel connected to you and the whole family. As such, some family meetings can consist entirely of games, songs, and other activities that enhance the connection among all family members in a spirit of light play.

Make it a part of your weekly schedule, or, if weekly seems too difficult to start, plan to have a meeting every two weeks or once a month. We have found that investing this time every week gives the best results, so it's worth making sacrifices elsewhere in your schedule to fit them in.

Have your meeting planned for thirty to forty-five minutes. You can always extend it to an hour or longer if time permits and everyone is having fun. Family meetings work best while sitting together—perhaps in a circle on your floor, rug, and chairs, or on sofas in an open spacious environment, but anywhere will work really.

Start With Sharing Appreciations

When it's time for the family meeting and everyone sits down, it's good to open with something that sets the tone for love and empathy. That's why we recommend always starting with Sharing Appreciations. Sharing Appreciations is a method whereby everyone takes a turn sharing something they appreciate about each person present.

There are only three requirements to Sharing Appreciations in the method we recommend.

The first one is that you give an appreciation to each person, and that everyone present does the same. The exception to this requirement is, of course, if one of the children feels so disconnected that he openly resists and defies Sharing Appreciations. In this case, it's better to quietly allow this person to skip his chance to Share Appreciations until he's ready. Eventually he'll discover that it's a joy and a source of pleasure to Share Appreciations.

If a child is resisting participating in the family meeting activities, it's far better to pay little attention to her resistance while continuing to have fun with everyone else. If this happens, continue to keep the door open for her to jump into the fun when she is ready. You can periodically invite her to join in. If a child resists the first time, after hearing another family member share, she may suddenly be ready to give her appreciations. If you put too much pressure on her to participate, it causes tension, and she may become "stuck" in that non-participatory stance. It's much easier for everyone if you just pay her mood little attention and show her through your example how much fun family meetings can be.

The second requirement of Sharing Appreciations is that when you give an appreciation to someone, you have to give it to them in the *first person*, speaking directly to them. Do not speak in the third person. *"What I appreciate about Daddy is how funny his jokes are."* Rather, you would speak directly to Daddy and say, *"What I appreciate about you, Daddy, is how you make me laugh with your jokes."*

The third requirement is that you don't use appreciations as a form of praise for something that may have tension, competition, or pressure attached to it. For example, you **don't** want to say to your daughter, *"Maggie, darling, I appreciate that* you have finally begun to hang your coat up when you get home," especially if you've been giving her a hard time about leaving her coat on the floor for months.

Always keep the tone **light** and **encouraging**. You can also give funny and sweet appreciations to make your child giggle, like, *"Maggie, darling, I appreciate it so much how you love to give your doll a pinch on the cheek just like you're the sweetest mama yourself, but I don't really understand why your doll likes to wear kiwi fruit for hats."*

Assigning Duties and Chores

Family meetings are great times to make changes to your routines. Children need to feel a sense of belonging and thrive when they feel they are participating as a fully competent and helpful part of the family. It gives children great joy and contributes to their sense of autonomy to feel as if they are a valuable member of the family "team."

However, to get to this, the child first needs to feel involved and empowered in the actual decision-making process around chores. When a child feels as if he holds the power of decision to help with chores, then he'll be less defiant about helping out.

A great way to do this is to make a list of all the chores that need to be done. You can even include things that only the adults can do, such as paying the bills or driving the vehicle to pick up groceries. Once the list of all the things that need to be done in the week in order for the family home to run smoothly is written down, then begin to assign the tasks to people.

For both of these steps, it's crucial to include everyone in the process. As the meeting facilitator, your job will be to strike the balance between initiating the next thing and allowing enough space for your children to participate in the process. If you tend to be more of an authoritarian parent, it may be harder for you to back off and let the other members of the family contribute ideas. On the other hand, if you tend to be more permissive, then your challenge may be to try to keep the meeting on track without letting your kids move the meeting away from where you wanted to go.

The end goal is to have everyone agree to do certain chores on the list. Having some tasks on the list that only adults can do prevents the children from taking some of your contributions for granted and opens the door for them to participate with the other chores.

After you have agreed to the division of the chores, if your child needs reminding about his commitment during the week, be sure to use gentle and Connective Communication to help encourage him into the chore.

> "Parents often believe that they have set up binding rules governing such items of conduct as cleanliness, orderliness, honesty, gentleness, and work ethic. Only if they themselves follow these rules will the child recognize them as obligations that hold good for everyone, and accept them as a matter of course. The essential rule is that the rules must be subject to no exceptions.
>
> Otherwise they will appear to the child NOT as necessary forms of a general social order, but as a scheme of unfair impositions."
>
> - Rudolf Dreikurs

Fun Activities During the Meetings

Embed culture and routines into your family meeting with a song, poem, passage, or perhaps by sharing a page from a favorite story. You could also start by playing the flute or some simple music.

It's nice to include an activity during your family meeting. Perhaps you could sing a song together that is a family favorite. You could also include some dance and movements. Some examples of good songs for younger kids are the "Elephant Dance" by Hap Palmer; or "Head, Shoulders, Knees, and Toes"; or "The Hokey Pokey"; or a finger-play song like "Eensy, Weensy Spider." Raffi is a great recording artist for kids who has all kinds of positive and fun songs as well.

You may want to enjoy a healthy snack or treat during family meeting time. You can even prepare, from scratch, cookies or a cake at the beginning of your meeting time as an activity. Then you can have it baking during the rest of the meeting so that you can enjoy it later.

Bringing Up Tough Issues

We recommend that when you begin to introduce family meetings into your regular weekly routines that at first you focus almost exclusively on building connection and having fun together. If you need to make any announcements that affect the family such as future or upcoming plans, new routines, a change in schedule, chores, or other issues that need discussion, it's best to focus on one issue at a time per meeting when you first start family meetings. After your meetings have become a part of your normal, family rituals, it becomes easier for children to process more issues per meeting.

If the meetings feel like a time where you're going to lecture your child or tell her the new rules, then the meetings will not have their desired effect because the child's needs for autonomy, connection, participation, and others will not be met.

When it is time to bring up issues, bring them up with lightness. If you feel too frustrated and worried about the issue, if you're in a bad mood, or if you're tense about the possible outcome, then save the issue for another time when you can bring it up tension-free. If you are feeling tense, then take your feelings to an Adult-to-Adult Listening Time session, as described in the previous chapter.

There are three primary needs that are met through Family Meetings: the need for autonomy, the need for participation, and the need for a sense of belonging. You can integrate activities that meet other needs too, such as the need for creative expression by singing, doing art, or playing games.

The need for autonomy is an important one to address when children act defiantly or inappropriately. The need for autonomy is met when children feel as if they have "choice" and "power." When children feel as if they are powerless and have no choice, then their need for autonomy may cause them to become very defiant, rebellious, and even aggressive. When children feel as if they do have choice and power in their lives, the majority of defiance melts. They will have nothing to rebel against if they feel like they are involved in making the choices in their lives. The more you trust in their good judgment, the more they will trust your direction.

Meeting a child's need for autonomy, participation, and belonging is really the key to transforming angry, rebellious kids into happy, helpful kids. When family meetings are introduced, older children or disconnected teens particularly may be very resistant, reluctant, and suspicious of your intentions. In this case, it's best to bring up only the tough issues well after a very good connection of trust and openness has been achieved by the other light, bonding activities you can play during family meetings.

Avoid blame and approach situations rather than persons

Try to bring up the tough issues by using neutral and non-blaming language. Instead of saying, *"Maggie, we need to find a solution to your problem of always leaving your coat on the floor,"* try saying it without accusation. Say something that keeps building on the connection that you're working on building during the meeting. Try something more along these lines, *"So we've already agreed that one thing we'd like to do more of during the week is go to the park and fly the kite. In order to do this, we need to get the entire house cleaning done early so that we can get to the park before dinner. I'll do the dishes and get the kitchen ready for dinner; what could you do to help us get out to the park in time?"*

Approaching the issues from a situation-centered perspective takes the blame and pressure off everyone and keeps the focus on the team's goals. When you single your child out for something, she feels isolated and disconnected from the group. Centering your attention on solving the needs of the team keeps everyone focused on proactive, win-win solutions, despite any mistakes or shortcomings. This avoids the pitfalls of making the problem something personal, rather than something situational. As soon as a problem becomes personal, disconnection happens, and all the energy that you're putting into the family meetings will go down the tubes.

In the example above, by keeping the conversation focused on situational solutions and giving room for your child to assert her autonomy, she may agree to clean up the other rooms while you get the kitchen ready. If the child got into the habit of cleaning up, she would likely come across her own coat on the floor at some point during their cleanup. She would then pick it up through her own volition, and eventually she would likely come to her own conclusion that it would be much better to try and remember to hang it up when she comes home. By coming to her own natural conclusion because of participating fully in the family, her "memory" for this kind of thing will improve dramatically!

Discussions, talking, sharing, and brainstorming are all great ways to create the atmosphere of creative and dynamic, situation-centered problem solving.

Growing Good Judgment

When trying to work out a win-win solution, give the example to your child of considering the consequences that affect everyone. If your child offers a solution, listen to it fully, be open and encouraging. This will demonstrate how much you trust in your child and how confident you are in his good thinking and judgment. When he sees this in you, he will begin to become more self-confident himself and begin to pay greater attention to approaching things with good judgment.

Sometimes when children offer their own solutions in family meetings, their solutions may still need a little more consideration before you make a decision based on it. But remember that your intention for the meeting is connection and encouragement. First, listen and genuinely acknowledge their good suggestion. Then, while reflecting on their good idea aloud, perhaps even repeating some of the benefits you see with their idea, bring up the considerations in a curious and light tone.

Here's an example: *"That's a great idea, sweetheart! I love your good ideas. If you help Mommy put away the dishes after dinner, it would help me complete the chores before bedtime. Then we would have more time to read stories before sleep. Oh! But how will you reach the top shelves to put away the dishes?"*

By encouraging the good thinking of your child towards a win-win solution for everyone, he will begin to feel more confident in his own judgment and abilities. This is a great way to openly support your child's intelligence. This approach will do away with a large portion of common childhood defiance and limit testing, especially regarding *family chores.*

Allow your children the time and space to figure out solutions. Usually they'll be very quick to express their ideas. By continually encouraging and posing questions along the way that keep them considering everyone and everything involved, they learn an incredible amount about creative problem solving and positive communication.

Try to avoid giving them the answer directly, and let them come up with the solution if they can. If they're having a hard time with the issue, then you can also help them out by offering easy-to-understand options. When offering options, it's good to start with two options to keep it simple. For example, you could say, *"Hmmm, let's see, maybe you could get the stool from the playroom? It's sturdy enough for the job. Or, instead, perhaps you could clear the dinner table and start your bath early?"*

It's worth mentioning that when it comes to chores and housework, be very careful not to pass on your own hurts from your childhood, especially if you were raised in an authoritarian family or environment. You may have residual stress around housework passed on by your parents. These feelings can literally last a lifetime if you don't work them out. If you can relate to this, then be very careful that you do not pass on these same feelings, resentments, and hurts about chores to your kids. In order to help work out these feelings, we recommend you schedule some Adult-to-Adult Listening Time so that you can approach housework from an entirely new and fresh perspective.

Closing the Meeting: Look Forward to Something

When the time is up and all the activities are complete, it's time to close the family meeting. You can close the meeting in any way that gives a sense of completion and maintains the connection.

You could sing a song, spend five minutes in silent meditation, or play a quick game. It's really up to you, and what we recommend is to close with sharing something that you're looking forward to. This is really a great way to close the family meeting and help solidify the bond created. What's nice is that it's similar to the opening appreciations. Doing something similar at the end really helps keep a tangible consistency that kids really eat up.

Each family member takes a turn to briefly share something that he or she is looking forward to in the week, month, or year ahead. It can be anything from a vacation, a holiday season, an event, meeting a friend, playing a game, watching a movie, going somewhere, or doing something simple. The only requirement is that you share something that you are genuinely looking forward to.

Ending on this note does several things. Firstly, it puts everyone into a very optimistic frame of mind about the future. Secondly, it increases the bonding by deepening the sharing. Finally, it moves everybody's attention from the interactions during the family meeting to upcoming events, which helps shift gears and brings everyone more into the present, which will aid in transitioning to another activity.

Throughout the Next Week

It's natural to expect your child to follow through after discussing issues in the family meetings, and you may also want to hold your child accountable to the agreements made. However, before you do, we suggest that you focus primarily on encouraging your child through patience, connection, and gentle repetition. Remember to respect your child's natural rhythm for learning.

Every child progresses and evolves different parts of his individuality at different rates. Some children advance verbally and intellectually very rapidly, while others develop great physical potential quite young. The same goes for integrating changes. Some children make transitions easier and faster, but the majority of them need more time for processing their experiences and transitions.

The approach we recommend during the week is that if your child takes a misstep and doesn't completely follow through with her end of the bargain, ***practice non-reaction*** before you say or do something. For example, if your child doesn't hang up her coat as she had agreed to do, instead of reprimanding your child, reminding her about it, or resentfully picking it up for her, just leave it there.

After a moment of ***not reacting***, you may conclude that it's a great opportunity to allow the Natural Consequences of her actions to unfold. You may just decide to leave her coat on the floor. You may discover to your pleasant surprise that a little later the coat is hung up. Sometimes all it takes is a little more time and a little more space for your child to change a bad habit.

If you had gotten upset or reprimanded your child because you found the coat on the floor, you would have stolen this great opportunity for her to learn. Getting upset and reprimanding your child only causes her to feel isolated and criticized, and consequently stresses her out, as we've discussed repeatedly in this book. Lecturing your child doesn't help her learn. Experience is your child's real teacher, as it is for all of us.

By applying patience and giving our kids the space and rhythm they need to process their own experiences, they are relieved of an incredible pressure to "keep up" with a fast-paced, adult world where they have no power and which doesn't make much sense to them.

The far better approach when your child makes a mistake, a misstep, or doesn't follow through with his end of the bargain is to simply and lightly come back to the issue the following week. During the next family meeting, just take some more time to re-think the matter together. This will encourage your child to give it further effort. Alternatively, in the example I just gave, you may find that your child just needed a little more time to get around to following through on the change.

Scheduling time every week for a family meeting can become a source of great happiness for you and your family. It's a very powerful and loving ritual that yields only positive results when used as we've described. It can also become a weekly event that everyone will look forward to. You can even plan special meals around it and make it a weekly family activity, a ritual to strengthen the bond between you and celebrate the love and good fortune you have for being together.

"Feelings of worth can flourish only in an atmosphere where individual differences are appreciated, mistakes are tolerated, communication is open, and rules are flexible — the kind of atmosphere that is found in a nurturing family."

- Virginia Satir

CHAPTER 14

NATURAL CONSEQUENCES

> *"Natural consequences represent the pressure of reality, without any specific action by parents, and are always effective."*
>
> *- Karen Owens*

Authoritarian and permissive parents often use "coercive consequences" as a way to coerce, threaten, and punish their children into cooperation. Logic and reason usually back up these kinds of consequences. They are sometimes referred to as "logical consequences." They are often used as a justification for strong-arming our children into compliance. These consequences do not engender equality nor respect.

Children naturally sense the unfairness of the situation and quickly model your example of manipulation. Their first defensive maneuvers against coercive consequences are defiance, rebellion, and stubbornness.

Natural Consequences, on the other hand, follow the democratic model of winning a child's cooperation through inclusion, connection, and respect. Natural Consequences do not make kids pay a harsh price for their mistakes. On the contrary, they help children gain knowledge, humility, and understanding through experiencing the repercussions of their actions in life.

How Can I Tell if the Consequences Are Natural or Coercive?

It is easy to tell if you are using coercive consequences or Natural Consequences with your child. All you have to do is gauge how involved you are in delivering the consequence.

With coercive consequences, the disciplinarian has to be actively involved in order to teach the child a lesson and dole out the consequence. However, coercion does not win cooperation. Children always see these kinds of consequences for what they are—a disguised form of punishment—and therefore rebel against it. This is why power struggles are so common where punishments and coercive consequences are used as disciplinarian methods.

Natural Consequences, on the other hand, require a "hands-off" approach. The parent has to step back and not interfere in the natural outcome of a child's choices and actions. Of course, the parent will always take the necessary action to ensure the child's full safety. Obviously, no parent will let a child discover the natural consequence of walking onto a busy highway.

The Natural Consequences that we are referring to in this chapter are safe opportunities for learning. They are used whenever the child can benefit from the challenge in front of him, with as little assistance from us as possible. You can easily discover the Natural Consequence to any decision by simply asking yourself,

"What would happen if I didn't interfere?"

It's an exercise in "allowing" your child to experience how his actions affect his life. It teaches him to become more practical and mindful in his choices, which increases his self-reliance, confidence, and autonomy.

As children learn to meet and solve the challenges that are in front of them, and as they discover creative and fun ways to work through the repercussions of their choices, they increase their practical adaptability, optimistic resilience, and ability to thrive in multiple circumstances.

"Freedom is not worth having if it does not include the freedom to make mistakes."

- Mahatma Gandhi

188

Using Connective Communication with Natural Consequences

Sometimes there is a fine line between coercive and Natural Consequences and the only differentiating factor may be how you communicate with your child. An example of this could be a situation where your child wants to watch TV and you want your child to finish cleaning her room and doing her homework. How you approach this situation may determine whether natural or coercive consequences are used. You can take the time before it's too late and patiently outline the plan to your child using inclusive "we" language, like this:

"Okay, darling, it's now 3 p.m., and we only have two and a half hours before dinner. I've got to do the laundry, clean the yard, and make a few phone calls before dinner, and you have to clean your bedroom and finish your homework. If you are able to complete those important things in time to watch some TV before dinner, then you may, just come get me before you turn on the TV so that I can make sure your room and homework are adequately completed."

Following this approach, the child receives very clear conditions about what the priorities are and knows that if she does not finish her chores in time, the natural consequence is that she will not have time to watch TV. Because you also mentioned that you need to "approve" the quality of her work before she turns on the TV, she will know that she cannot simply rush through her duties; if she does, the natural consequence will be that she will have to make the necessary improvements before she can begin her TV watching.

Using this same example, if you did not take the time to outline the plan and communicate the needs of the afternoon with your child, you may have said instead, *"How many times have*

I told you that you can't watch TV until your room is clean and your homework complete." Because this response is personally directed, rather than focused on the situation, the child will not feel a sense of participation and belonging in the order of the family. It's likely that she will then resent her chores and feel as if you are just trying to control her and may try to rush through it without regard for quality just to get to the TV faster.

As a result, you may feel inclined to reprimand your child for a job poorly done when you see that her room is not satisfactorily tidy. You may be inclined to turn off the TV and tell her to finish cleaning her room. Even though your actions may seem like the logical consequence to her poor cleaning efforts, the child will likely put up a fuss and increase her dislike for chores and her resentment of your authority. The point here is that when it comes to tidying her room, consequences are not the best form of discipline. What would be more effective is to use limit setting with Connective Communication.

Let's look at an example of using Connective Communication with Natural Consequences for a toddler. Let's say a toddler spills a large container of juice all over the floor. Because the child is so young, he's not able to deal with this consequence all by himself; he will need your help. The first thing you may likely do is jump in to help contain the mess from growing.

When to Set Limits and When to Allow Natural Consequences

The requirement for successful implementation of Natural Consequences is that the parent, or teacher, must be in a state of *clear thinking* and *good judgment*. That way you can have the sensitivity to reach a good balance between expecting too much from your child and expecting too little. You need the clarity of mind to make a good choice between using Natural Consequences and *setting limits*.

In essence, Natural Consequences are the limits set by reality, not set by you.

When your child is in school, he will discover the Natural Consequences of his actions for himself, based on the social mores, school culture, and academic curriculum.

There are many reasons why bullying is awful, but one key reason is that it acts as a natural consequence to their zest, innocence, and intelligence. When a bright child suffers at the hands of a bully as a consequence of how he is shining, this is an example of coercive consequences used to dominate in order to capture the attention of their peers. Here the *bullying* is a result of an attention-starved child who dominates other children in order to feel power and control attention. The bully is usually motivated by unmet needs of full attention and autonomy.

> "While we are free to choose our actions, we are not free to choose the consequences of our actions."
>   - Stephen R. Covey

Using Natural Consequences to Inspire Cleanliness and Order

Natural Consequences are very effective to teach children to respect cleanliness and appreciate order. Let's consider the example that your child doesn't hang up his wet bathing suit after swimming. You can remind him, you can scold him, you can hang it up for him, or you can do nothing and leave it there.

The natural consequence of leaving something on the floor is that it stays on the floor until someone picks it up. The permissive parent often tends to pick up after their child—all the time. The natural consequence of using permissive discipline in trying to keep a house clean is that the child's lack of participation creates an apathetic approach to cleanliness. Luckily, this is easily cured through increasing the child's participation in family cleaning and chores.

The authoritarian parent doesn't have any trouble increasing the child's participation in chores; they have trouble maintaining it without a power struggle. They may yell at or reprimand the child for leaving the bathing suit on the floor. They rely on enforcing rules of order by using coercive consequences such as withholding privileges or allowance, or more severe punishments. The child rebels by avoiding responsibility or openly defying them.

However, the use of Connective Communication, family limits, loving limits, Play Attention Time, and Natural Consequences, meets children's needs for participation, belonging, autonomy, attention, and security. When a child's needs are met and his attention is clear, he is incredibly helpful and generously contributive to various family challenges. Even if you think your child will be resistant to more chores and participation, you'll be surprised how his attitude transforms through this democratic approach.

So, the natural consequence of a child leaving his wet swim suit on the floor is that next time he goes swimming, he will have to put on a wet bathing suit. The uncomfortable experience of putting on a wet bathing suit will make any child remember why hanging our clothes to dry is a good idea. This experiential knowledge will do more to help him develop habits of cleanliness, order, and responsibility better than a dozen lectures.

How to Help Your Child Learn From Natural Consequences

Most often, you don't have to do anything to help your child learn from Natural Consequences, she will learn all by herself. When your child faces the natural consequence of her actions, she may not make much of a fuss about it.

Avoid the temptation of using it as a teaching aid or a "told you so" opportunity or "rubbing it in" in any way. Let children integrate the experience at their own rate. Just as it takes babies many falls before they learn how to walk with confidence, so too does it sometimes take many mistakes and missteps to master a new habit.

However, at times it may be quite appropriate to assist your child with the consequence. If your child asks for your help, or asks you questions in dealing with the consequence, then by all means, offer your assistance as you deem appropriate.

Upon assessing the situation, you may deem the best response is simply to offer some encouragement, or maybe you will discover that all your child needs is some information that could be useful in dealing with the consequence more intelligently. If your child spills a large container of juice all over the floor, she may reach for a paper towel to clean it up. While this is a perfectly good idea, it's also a waste because it would take more than a full roll to clean up such a mess. You could assist your child in this case by suggesting she use the mop instead.

Sometimes the consequence may also be more than they can handle, and this is a great opportunity to jump in to help them wholeheartedly. It is also a good opportunity to model a team-focused and helpful attitude. Teaching children how to be genuinely and generously helpful without being smothering or domineering is a great gift for children and parents. Because when you are old, feeble, and in need of help, your children will treat you with the same love and respect with which you are raising them.

By allowing the natural consequence to unfold in the daily lives of children, their ability to handle challenges and prevent unnecessary difficulties will greatly increase. Children given this responsibility in an age-appropriate way become much more participatory in the family routines and chores. Facing the Natural Consequences of your actions quickly teaches the benefits of doing things in efficient ways.

"While we try to teach our children all about life, it is our children who teach us what life is all about."

- Angela Schwindt

SUGAR AND
NOT EVERYTHING NICE

> *"The terrible twos are a myth! Mood swings, the inability to concentrate, temper tantrums, and the most significant—low self-esteem are all the effects of too much sugar in your child's diet."*
>
> *- Kathleen DesMaisons*

study conducted by the University of South Carolina found that children who display hyperactive tendencies tend to become more destructive and restless when their blood sugar is high. Additional studies have found that aggressive and challenging behaviors in children often come about when children consume too much sugar. This is only one of the reasons why limiting your child's sugar consumption is one of the best choices you can make.

With childhood obesity and diabetes increasing around the world at alarming rates, parents and health care officials are now paying much more attention to the foods and drinks we give to kids. Kathleen DesMaisons, author of *Little Sugar Addicts*,[14] has studied the correlation among sugar, health, and child behavior for more than fifteen years. Her studies confirm what many mothers already intuitively knew: sugar affects our children's moods.

"The terrible twos are a myth!" says DesMaisons, stating that terrible-two behaviors can be a direct result of having too much sugar. She continues, *"Mood swings, the inability to concentrate, temper tantrums, and the most significant—low self-esteem are all the effects of too much sugar in your child's diet."*

As any parent knows, limiting sugar in this day and age is not always easy. The modern diet that is marketed and sold commercially to children and parents more often than not includes sugary cereals, sugary snacks, sugary drinks, and sugary treats. Additionally, foods that are primarily refined carbohydrates, such as white bread, white pasta, instant rice, crackers, cookies, and many kinds of cereals, also considerably spike blood sugar levels. This spike in blood sugar is known as a glycemic reaction. This happens because refined carbohydrates transform into sugar almost instantly through the digestive process.

When you have high blood sugar levels, your body will have difficulty metabolizing the amino acids and essential nutrients that it also needs. Additionally, excessively high blood sugar contributes to many inflammatory health problems. High blood sugar can also lead to diabetes, allergies, poor attention, hyperactivity, tooth decay, digestive problems, a weakened immune system, and a host of inflammatory illnesses.

---

14 (DesMaisons, 2004)

The problem is that kids love simple carbohydrates and sweet foods, so they will eat as much of them as they can. Biology is partly to blame. Because they're growing so rapidly and they expend so much energy during the day, their bodies and brains require a higher ratio of sugar in their diet than adults do. Obviously, sugar is necessary to our survival; there is nothing "bad" about it—we actually need it! The key is, as with most things, balance and moderation. If children are fed too much refined sugar, they may develop diabetes or obesity, or many other health problems.

Refined sugar refers to the white sugar commonly used in most commercial sweets and desserts. White sugar is nutritionally empty and has zero benefits besides its caloric value. However, raw sugar cane, from which white sugar is refined, is very healthy and rich in anti-oxidants, minerals, vitamins, and nutrients.

You want to want to avoid refined forms of sugar and instead choose foods that digest into sugar more slowly and naturally. These foods tend to nourish your children's cells much better and give them more even, stable, and consistently thriving energy. The simplest way to avoid refined sugars is to reduce its availability in your home. You can replace these products with healthier options, which can be just as delicious, if not more. There are many low-sugar sweeteners and healthy, low-sugar breakfasts, snacks, and desserts available that kids love.

Unfortunately, most commercial products marketed for kids have refined sugar added to them in order to make them more appealing. You will commonly see Latin names for other kinds of sugars in the ingredient lists of items in the grocery store. Sugar also goes by the name of glucose, dextrose, lactose, fructose, sucrose, corn syrup, caramel, galactose, maltose, and other names that end in "ose."

You'll also often see it listed as icing sugar, brown sugar, cane sugar, granulated sugar, powdered sugar, and other names. Look for these names on the ingredient labels of items you buy. It's commonly added to baked goods, pancake and baking mixes, drinks, juices, pop, yogurts, peanut butter, cereals, breads, crackers, cookies, snacks, granola bars, canned soups, canned or packaged fruit, bottled pasta sauce, flavored milk, and many, many other items in the grocery store. Even some fast food chains, like McDonald's, use white sugar in their hamburgers to make them tastier.

Dealing With Cultural and Social "Sugar Pressure"

People often offer lollipops, cookies, and other sweets to children. We understand that many people don't realize that too much sugar can be a problem. You can always try to take the sweet gift before your child has a chance to grab it. You can also smile, thank them, and tell them that you'll save it for later as he already had enough sugar for the day.

When you decline an offer with a sincere smile and polite explanation, people usually are quite understanding and not offended. Sometimes this situation is more difficult with family members, but it doesn't have to be. Just be sure to remain polite and communicative with your family members, just as you would with anyone. It does happen in some cases that with families, even politeness and openness isn't always enough to change old relationship habits.

Connective Communication

After all, you are the parent; you have the final say in what goes for your child. In fact, your child is depending on you to make the best decisions on his behalf. If a baby or a ten-year-old eats candy all day, it is not his fault that he may suffer health problems from this. The parents are the ones responsible for ensuring their child's health is always cared for.

You don't need to explain to your family members the reasons, the statistical proof, or the rationale behind your decision to limit your child's sugar consumption. You can just say, *"We've decided to feed him less sugar,"* or *"We've found that his behavior is better when he doesn't eat too much sugar."* It's as simple as that.

What is the Glycemic Index and What Does it Have to Do With Sugar?

The glycemic index (GI)[15] is the measure of the amount of carbohydrates in your food that raise your blood sugar levels. Foods with a glycemic index of 70 and above are considered high. These are carbohydrate-rich foods that break down quickly during digestion, thereby releasing glucose (sugar) rapidly into the bloodstream.

Low GI foods, which break down more slowly, release glucose more gradually into the bloodstream, and thereby provide the body with the nourishment it needs without the inflammatory effects of high blood sugar levels. Common low GI foods are minimally processed and refined foods that are still close to their natural form, such as brown rice, whole grain breads, raw nuts, and fibrous vegetables.

_____

15 http://en.wikipedia.org/wiki/Glycemic_index

To moderate blood sugar and reduce calories, you can simply replace high GI meals with tasty, low GI alternatives. We don't recommend the "no sugar diet" because it's easier to accept change when it's gradual. Children thrive on new experiences, so long as they feel included in the new experience and their needs for connection and autonomy are met, then a change in food habits may not be so difficult to implement in your family routine.

Instead of high GI snacks such as cake and spaghetti, try whole grain pasta salad or fruit. Instead of dried fruit leathers, which have a higher GI, give your child a fresh apple. Instead of a granola bar, offer your child a banana. Instead of crackers and cheese, offer your child cucumber and fresh nuts. Instead of store-bought cookies, bake your own with molasses or honey.

Setting Sugar Limits

As hard as we try to make transitions and changes go smoothly, our children still often show resistance. Sometimes they put up a real fuss. They may even refuse to eat much then complain about being hungry. This is often their way of testing this new food limit. As long as you make plenty of healthy and delicious foods readily accessible and maintain a kind limit with the food, they will soon give up their big show, seeing that their antics will get them nowhere.

If you make a big deal about their eating, then the pressure and tension around food and eating only increases, giving further fuel to their defiant cause. The democratic approach is not to sway them with pleas, bribes, rewards, threats, or punishments, but to let them experience the natural consequence of their choice, which in this case would be hunger.

Through Natural Consequences and maintaining a loving connection with your children as you remain firm in this new food limit, they soon discover that there is no power in their defiance, and eventually settle into these new habits of eating as their attention is eventually drawn to other things.

There are times when emotional tension and stress result in fussy eating. If this is the case, then limiting sugar may be the catalyst to having a big emotional tantrum and healing. At this point, you would practice setting a Healing Limit to allow all the tension to drain fully.

Try a Taste of Something New

By replacing unhealthy and over-sweetened foods with delicious, healthy options, your family will eventually begin to thrive and devour your cooking with delight. Sometimes though, when you prepare new things, your child may not even want to taste it. A great way to help overcome this issue is to introduce what we call a "Try a Taste" tradition in your home.

A Try a Taste tradition becomes a dining rule where everyone in the family has to try two full bites of anything served. After two full bites, if they don't prefer to continue eating it, they may leave that portion of their food. To get your child's cooperation on this, you may find family meetings helpful. Given the right opportunity, you may simply be able to introduce it in a fun and light way during dinner. If presented in the right way and at the right time, your child will most likely go along with this new tradition.

So when your child doesn't want to try something he is served, you simply say, *"Sweetie, if you're not sure about something on your plate, remember to try a taste."*

By using this language, you place no pressure on your child and you build no tension. The response is non-emotional, yet connected and encouraging him towards a solution that is in his best interest.

Suppose he replies by saying, *"No! I don't want to try a taste! It's yucky!"* Then this indicates that you may need to set a kind verbal limit by saying, *"Sweetie, remember that we don't talk that way about our food. It's fine if you're not sure about it. I can understand. If you don't want to eat it, just try two tastes and then you can decide."* With this response, you're setting a limit on how he expresses manners and etiquette, while still not reacting to the content of his behavior.

Healthy Sweeteners and Sugar Alternatives

Here are some sugar alternatives you can use instead of refined (white) sugar:

1. Stevia
2. Blackstrap molasses (also a great natural source of vitamin B)
3. Honey (also has benefits for the immune system)
4. Real maple syrup
5. Natural cane sugar
6. Natural date syrup

Stevia is our top recommended sugar alternative because it has zero calories, zero carbs, is gluten free, and is 40 to 300 times as sweet as sugar—depending on what kind you buy. Additionally, studies have found that lowering blood pressure and blood sugar aids calcium formation. Stevia has even been found to contain antibacterial properties, which can help against candida, allergies, and respiratory issues.

What About Synthetic, Chemical and Artificial Sweeteners?

The most commonly sold synthetic and artificial sweeteners are aspartame, saccharin, sucralose, acesulfame-k (ace-k), neotame, and there are surely more coming out. They are known on the market as Splenda®, Sweet N Low®, Sweet One®, Sunett®, Equal®, and NutraSweet®.

The National Cancer Institute in America reported that studies in laboratory rats during the early 1970s linked saccharin with the development of bladder cancer. For this reason, the American Congress mandated that further studies of saccharin be performed. It also required that all food containing saccharin bear the following warning label: *"Use of this product may be hazardous to your health. This product contains saccharin, which has been determined to cause cancer in laboratory animals."* [16]

The United States Food and Drug Administration (FDA)[17] states that studies thus far have not proven these substances to be significantly dangerous to humans. Therefore, they remain on the market in many low-calorie and "diet" food products. Our opinion is to keep it simple and as close to natural as possible when it comes to feeding the bodies of our children.

Not so long ago we thought there was nothing wrong with spraying DDT (dichlorodiphenyltrichloroethane) and other poisonous pesticides in residential neighborhoods, but DDT was banned in 1972 after years of use when enough research proved it to be a deadly nerve poison.

While the research on synthetic sweeteners is not yet as conclusive as DDT, why take a risk on a newly marketed chemical

16 (Soffritti, Belpoggi, Espoti, & Lambertini, 2005)
17 (Anonymous, FDA Statement on European Asparthame Study, 2006)

patent when there are healthy, time-tested, natural alternatives that you can grow in your own garden?

Using stevia, honey, blackstrap molasses, and natural cane sugar in recipes that call for sweeteners, while offering your child more healthy alternatives to foods and snacks that have a low glycemic index, can help your child overcome a lot of challenging behavior and health issues.

"We are indeed much more than what we eat, but what we eat can nevertheless help us to be much more than what we are."

- Adelle Davis

CHAPTER 16

EXERCISE IS A NEED

"A bear, however hard he tries, grows tubby without exercise."

- Winnie the Pooh

*T*he best kind of exercise for children is aerobic exercise that includes muscular strengthening, stretching, hand-eye coordination, and induces the need for balance and spatial awareness. Increased benefits are derived from social exercise that involves other people.

The more fun, light, and playful exercise is, the better. When exercise is done outside in a free play environment, even more benefits are achieved. From swimming, competitive sports, climbing, and team games to running, tag, bouncing, and climbing, children love getting good exercise in the fresh air when given the opportunity.

When children engage regularly in exercise, their concentration, problem solving abilities, memory, mood, behavior, and overall health and demeanor will dramatically improve. Exercise is

especially good for kids who exhibit hyperactive tendencies as it provides a healthy outlet for their restlessness high energy.

How Exercise Affects Your Child's Behavior

Just like a wild animal in a small cage, children will run in circles if confined indoors too long without room to run freely and fresh air to breathe deeply. Urban living situations in many parts of the world can sometimes make it a challenge for children to get adequate exercise because the typical apartment complex offers no space for them to run around freely. In modern suburban developments, playgrounds are often installed, making exercise more accessible.

Even so, modernization and consumerism have built shopping malls to replace parks and fields. Common childhood activities now include isolation with the television and video games instead of running around outside and playing with the other kids in the neighborhood. The International Obesity Task Force currently estimates that 22 million children worldwide under five years old suffer from morbid obesity![18]

*22,000,000 **children worldwide under five years old suffer from morbid obesity!***

As far back as 1986, research by Gruber[19]showed that exercise among elementary-age children leads to healthier self-esteem. Exercise teaches children self-control and focus, which can help to give them a better sense of personal capability. The Medical College of Georgia found that twenty to forty minutes of hula-hooping and jump rope every day improved thinking and brain capability among kids between the ages of seven and eleven.

---

18 International Obesity Taskforce. http://www.iotf.org/childhoodobesity.asp
19 (Gruber, 1985)

Aerobic exercise, in particular, is indispensable. The California Department of Education[20] found that those deemed fit through aerobic exercise scored twice as well as those deemed unfit. Charles Hillman of the University of Illinois also related aerobic capacity to better attention, memory, and processing speed.[21] This is because aerobic exercise improves the delivery of oxygen and blood in the body, including the brain, helping it function better.

Ever heard the old adage "exercise makes people happy"? Well, there's more fact than fiction to it. Studies by Smits, Berry, Rosenfield, and colleagues found that exercise is an effective cure for depression and anxiety in both adults and children.[22]

Furthermore, people who exercise regularly are less sensitive to anxiety reactions, which help them function better. This is because exercise improves the transmission of the chemicals norepinephrine and serotonin in the brain.[23] Norepinephrine and serotonin are neurotransmitters that are essential in regulating mood.

There Is Magic Outside

The outdoors is good for your physical and mental health. Exercise outside has twice the benefits of indoor exercise, not only because of the fresh oxygen and Vitamin D you get from the sun, but also because nature has a calming and revitalizing effect. Being in a green or natural setting, seeing butterflies, bugs, birds, animals, and live plants can invigorate and inspire children with wonder and joy.

---

20 (Group, 2009)
21 (Hillman)
22 (Smits, Berry, Rosenfield, Powers, Behar, & Otto, 2008)
23 (Ransford, 1982)

Researchers Frances E. Kuo and Andrea Faber Taylor, who published their findings in the *American Journal of Public Health*, found that green or natural settings helped reduce symptoms of Attention Deficit Hyperactivity Disorder (ADHD) in children.[24] They gave kids the same game to play indoors and outdoors, and the children were more calm and relaxed when they played outdoors. A 2005 study called "Leave No Child Inside" funded by the Sierra Club of California also found that children in outdoor classrooms improved their science scores by 27 percent.[25]

Jim Byford of the University of Tennessee believes that the outdoors is more relaxing because outside play allows kids to be more creative and less structured. Games played outdoors have the necessary self-directed quality that children need from their playtime.[26] We covered this type of play extensively in the Self-Directed Play chapter.

How to Help Your Child Exercise More

We recommend that children enjoy a minimum of one hour of moderate to rigorous physical activity each day. Of course, there may be times when your little one is under the weather and needs rest over exercise, so parental discretion is always advised. Children who have gotten into the habit of being lazy may resist getting off the couch at first, so you have to make the exercise fun. There are two main options you can pursue: exercise at home with the family, or enroll your child in a program, extra-curricular activity, or a sport team.

---

24 (Taylor, Kuo, & Sullivan, 2001)
25 (Anonymous, Leave No New Mexico Child Inside, 2007)
26 (Byford)

Exercise at home with the family

You can do all kinds of fun things at home in your neighborhood or you can even go on an excursion. You can go for a bicycle ride, go to a playground, climb on monkey bars, go jogging, or run around together. You can play games such as tag, catch, Frisbee, tennis, badminton; you can build snow forts in the winter; or you can play soccer or football. You can even go for a hike, go canoeing, or go swimming at a beach. The choices are virtually endless. Whatever you do, make sure you get outside, move your body, and, most importantly, have plenty of fun!

Enroll your child in a club or sports program

More important than the convenience of location and the type of program you choose is the quality of the program leader, coach, or teacher. Be sure to spend plenty of time observing and assessing the way the teachers and coaches interact with the children, both individually and as a team. Make sure these teachers are warm and passionate about what they're doing. Also, be sure that their passion isn't greater than their sensitivity and care of your children.

You should always use encouragement instead of critical discipline. Coaches or teachers who try to coax children by criticizing them, comparing them, or making fun of them will only succeed in hurting the child's self-esteem.

Luckily, there are plenty of wonderfully gifted and generous people who teach and lead children's sports programs and activities. In many urban settings, you can find groups that your child can attend for gymnastics, soccer, martial arts, bicycling, swimming, track and field, team sports, dancing, rock climbing, outdoor programs, horse riding, and even Capoeira.

211

Competitive Sports and Games

Some children really thrive in competitive environments, while others do not, so be aware of your child's needs and particularly their age. Young children under the age of six may have a hard time with "losing" or being "out" in a game, although after some direction and teaching, they will surely understand how it works. When playing these games with young children, be aware that when they "lose" or they are "out" in a game, their sense of connection is broken, and it can cause some tension for them.

However, this is not always the case, and some young children remain enthusiastically connected to the rest of the kids and game even if they are sitting on the sidelines after being called "out." This will depend a lot on the individual personality and needs of the child. There are some great programs like the *Awareness Through The Body*[27] initiative in South India that actually includes exercises that call for kids to meditate on how they feel when they lose in a game and also how they feel when they win in a game.

These kinds of programs have incredible success with giving children confidence and clarity of mind despite apparent failures and mistakes. Sometimes, if children feel embarrassed about their physical capacities, if a more agile or athletic peer criticizes their ability, or if they have their zest crushed by a sense of failure, they may be hesitant or even outright against the idea of getting exercise.

If this is the case, you can use Natural Giggles, Play Attention Time, Self-Directed Play, or setting limits to connect with your

---

27 http://awarenessthroughthebody.com/

child first. Once the connection is strong enough, then initiate exercise in a way that is fun and that maintains the connection.

Exercising With Your Child Creates Memories

I remember a time when I was driving to visit some family with my son and he was feeling a little carsick. I knew of a nice nature trail on the way, so we stopped next to a beautiful place to hike up an escarpment. I encouraged him to go for a walk as I knew some fresh air and a little exercise would revitalize him.

At first, he resisted it and just wanted to sit on a large rock outside the car because he seemed to be still feeling a little carsick. I waited until he was ready to move a bit more. After about two minutes, he started to move around, and I said to him, "Let's just go for a little walk and see something neat."

This no-pressure language piqued his interest and curiosity, so he agreed but said he didn't want to go far. As we started down the path, I started to skip, jump, and engage him in some running play. Before we knew it, we were running down the trail together, and we soon started rock climbing up the cliffs of the hill until we finally came upon a view of the wide, lush valley below us. We were both flushed, sweaty, and flashing bright smiles and feeling connected, revitalized, and happy.

After that time, my son always wanted to go back to this place because it was so much fun, and we still return there frequently for some amazing exercise that is both outdoors and fun.

Exercising with your child can bring you many precious memories while keeping you extremely fit! Who needs a personal trainer when you have a child?

213

"Those who think they have not time for bodily exercise will sooner or later have to find time for illness."

- Edward Stanley

CHAPTER 17

SMART SLEEP

> *"Sleep is the golden chain that ties health and our bodies together."*
>
> *- Thomas Dekker*

*S*leep is essential for your child's mental, emotional, and physical health. The quality and quantity of sleep is important to your child's behavior, sharpness of mind, and overall mood. Getting enough sleep keeps us healthy, optimistic, and smart. According to the *New England Journal of Medicine*, half of all American children are estimated to suffer from inadequate sleep.[28]

A team of scientists at Northwestern University found that sleep affected the behavior in two- and three-year-old children. Those who slept fewer than ten hours in a twenty-four-hour period consistently showed more opposition, non-compliance, and aggressive behaviors.[29]

---

28 (Selman, 2005)
29 (Reid, 2002)

A growing child will thrive best with ten to fourteen hours of sleep each night. This will allow their growing bodies the necessary cellular generation that children need during sleep. Children need more sleep than adults do, not only because they are growing, but also because they are building new antigens (immune defenses) against all kinds of bugs and bacteria that they have never been exposed to before. Adults, on the other hand, already have dozens of years building their antigen defenses against microbial invaders.

A recent Finnish study suggested that short sleep duration, even without sleeping difficulties, increases the risk for behavioral symptoms and symptoms of ADHD in children. Finnish researcher Juulia Paavonen, MD, PhD said, "We were able to show that short sleep duration and sleeping difficulties are related to behavioral symptoms of ADHD, and we also showed that short sleep, per se, increases behavioral symptoms, regardless of the presence of sleeping difficulties."[30]

Getting Adequate Sleep

Considering these studies, how can we help our children get adequate sleep, particularly when some children have a hard time going to sleep early or staying soundly asleep?

There are three things that help make sleep easier. First is a good bedtime routine, second is a good morning routine, and third is making sure that all of your child's needs are met and they don't have any unprocessed tension or stress.

Bedtime Routine

A good bedtime routine works very well to get children to sleep on time because children thrive within routines they can

---

30 (Paavonen, et al., 2009)

anticipate. Routines are to children what the earth is to plants; they are something into which children can sink their roots and gain stability and security. Routines provide a foundational framework for children to develop their character, pace, confidence, and worldview.

Routines consist of two factors: time and space. Time refers to the pace and rhythm of the routines. Space refers to the external environment and physical location where the routines are performed. We see how routines are followed in our schools in a very systematic way. Time is structured from the beginning to the end of school: length of classes, length of breaks between classes, as well as how much time is given to write tests and perform examinations. The space refers to the physical structure, size, and organization of the school and classrooms, as well as the location in the community.

When considering sleep, we need to take a look at the time and space of our current routines. Primarily, we have to consider the needs of our children regarding the right balance of stimulation. Too much stimulation and they get wired and distracted; too little stimulation and they get bored and bounce off the walls. Time refers to the pace and schedule that we set up in our home and our children's lives. The pace of busy, modern living often over-stimulates children to the point that they are wired and can't sleep well.

Given a little more down time to process the activity of their day, these children often will calm down considerably and sleep much better. Giving them "down time" means time that has zero stimulation. No TV, no radio, no video games, no friends, just quiet and unstructured time for them to do whatever they want without stimulating themselves further.

Scheduling thirty to sixty minutes a day where your child can just relax at home and process their busy day will do wonders to free up their attention and calm their bodies and their minds. This will not only help them sleep better at night, but it also gives them a chance to come to peace with experiences that may have otherwise festered in the back of their minds. While scheduling some down time in the day doesn't necessarily have to be part of the bedtime routine, it will in fact make your child much more participatory when it comes time to get ready for bed.

One of the simplest ways to help your child sleep better at night is to put them to bed earlier. Most children will tend to wake up at the same time, so putting them to bed earlier will help them get more sleep. However, it may take some time for your child to get used to a new sleep pattern. At first, he may not fall asleep right away, but if you provide your child with enough exercise during the day and not too much stimulation, he may very well begin falling asleep earlier without any hitch.

You may have to make some adjustments in your family routine in order to get your child to bed earlier. You may need to start dinner earlier, or you may even need to change your working situation or your family schedule. You may even cancel some extra-curricular activities in order to get your child to bed on time. Realize that these changes may not seem so simple and easy, but giving your child's body the opportunity to sleep more while it's growing and developing will be a huge gift that will benefit your child for life.

The key to developing an effective bedtime routine is to have multiple activities that lead to the bedtime. When these activities build a sense of connection with your child, he will likely go along with them and fall asleep much easier. Here's an example of a routine you can follow starting with the time your child returns from school.

A BEDTiME ROUTiNE EXAMPLE:

4:00 p.m.	Arrive home from school
4:00-4:30 p.m.	After school healthy snack—avoid sugary foods. Give cucumber, carrots, apples, or other vegetables or fruits.
4:30-5:00 p.m.	Quiet time with no stimulation, where your child can just relax on the couch, on the bed, or anywhere in the house and do anything that is not too stimulating.
5:00-5:45 p.m.	Play time
5:45-6:00 p.m.	Help set the table for the family dinner
6:00-6:45 p.m.	Dinner
6:45-7:00 p.m.	Family cleanup time: this gives your child an opportunity to feel connected with the family by helping put the dishes away or any other cleanups before bed.
7:00-7:30 p.m.	Get ready for bed: this can include bathing, brushing teeth, putting on pajamas, etc.
7:30-8:00 p.m.	Bedtime story time: Tuck your child into bed by reading some happy storybooks. This is relaxing and builds a connection with you.
8:00 p.m.	Lights out and kiss goodnight

This is just an example of a schedule that moves in a linear progression towards bedtime while meeting your child's needs for connection, participation, information, play, appropriate stimulation, relaxation, and healthy nutrition. With this routine, your child will likely be asleep by 8:30 p.m., which will give her ten hours of sleep if she wakes up at 6:30 a.m.

A Happy Child Sleeps Well

For the sake of clarity, let's define "happy" as a child who has all his needs met and is tension free. Children and babies who tend to have a hard time falling asleep or staying asleep usually have some unmet needs. As we just described, it may be that they need less stimulation and some quiet time to process their active experiences. Perhaps they may also need more physical exercise to help their bodies relax at night. Often, children may have lingering tension, pressure, or stress that keeps their minds active at night.

Insomnia has become a major issue in modern society. Every year more adults seek ways to sleep better. This issue is often due to excessive stimulation during the day, an overactive mind, not enough exercise, and an accumulation of stress. For example, the University of Auckland found that young children need an extra three minutes to fall asleep for every hour they spend sitting inactive during the day. More importantly, kids who fall asleep faster sleep better and longer. This is why it's so important to take some time to really assess the needs of your child and determine whether tension or stress may be involved.

As adults, we know that when we are stressed about something, our sleep can be easily disturbed. Children are just the same, although what tends to stress children are not the same things that worry adults. The chapter on stress in this book goes into much detail on this.

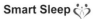

Morning Routine

Not only does a morning routine get your day off to a good start, but it's also a big part of the sleep formula. Many parents and families rush like crazy in the morning to get out of the house on time, which sets the tone for the day to be rushed and stressed. By getting to bed earlier, you've already won half the battle of making the morning a more welcoming transition from the passivity of sleep into the activity of daytime. Early to bed also makes it easier to get up early in the morning, thus giving you more time to get out of the house on time.

Here are a few good tips to make the morning routine of getting up, ready, and out of the door more harmonious:

1. **Wake up earlier.** Rushing and stressing out about getting to school and work on time will consume more energy than thirty minutes worth of sleep will provide. So wake up fifteen, thirty, forty-five minutes or even an hour earlier if you need to. Waking your child up earlier will also help sleepy heads wake up and get ready in time for school.

2. **Have plenty of time for breakfast.** Making a healthy breakfast doesn't take that much time. Cooking oatmeal doesn't take more than twenty minutes, and many other healthy breakfasts can be prepared quickly. Breakfast is a very important meal because it gives your child the energy to thrive during the first part of the day. Many children may not be so hungry when they first wake up because they're tired. Sweet breakfasts usually motivate them to eat, but as we discussed in the chapter on sugar, these breakfasts don't provide them with the sustainable energy they need.

Often, if you give your children more time to wake up, they will have more time to notice their appetite and eat a nice breakfast. In addition, many children will develop the habit of having a bowel movement in the morning before having breakfast. It's important to give your children plenty of time to do their business in the bathroom, which will help them keep their digestive system in great shape. Rushing them to finish going to the bathroom or pushing them to eat faster can sometimes have harmful effects later on, leading to constipation, incomplete bowel movements, or eating disorders.

3. **Keep your child on track with gentle reminders.** As the morning routine develops into a proper routine, your child will begin to stay on track because he will know what he has to do in the morning to get ready and leave. To begin with, you may have to keep your child on track with gentle reminders. These are just verbal communications to let your child know what he has to do next and to help nudge him along if he ends up lagging at any point.

   For example, if your child has taken a little longer to get to the breakfast table and eat in the morning, you can say something like, "All right, sweetie, we have to leave in ten minutes, so once you finish your meal, we'll have to get your coat on and go." This tone is not rushing, nor stressful. The language here follows the Connective Communication principles by keeping the focus on the situation, not on the child, and by using "we" when talking about the timeline.

4. **If you tend to be late and to rush out the house, then plan to leave ten minutes early.** It's crucial to continue giving your child gentle reminders as she gets ready to

keep moving her along,   particularly if your child tends to put up a fuss or lag behind in the morning. You may even decide to give yourself more than ten extra minutes. This is something you can test and adjust as you go.

5. **Practice**. Developing new routines takes time to integrate and get right. It may take days, weeks, or months to get the morning routines working smoothly and flawlessly. You may even need to make adjustments in your daily commitments and schedules to make them work. Perhaps the first few times you try a new morning routine it works flawlessly, then a few days later your child throws a big tantrum in the morning.

Parenting is like a wilderness adventure. As with any adventure, we need to prepare ourselves by mapping the course. Yet, despite all our preparations, we never know how the weather will turn out. As the old adage says, "Man plans and God laughs." Whether you are religious or not, you can surely relate as a parent. So whether the routine goes smoothly at first, or your first attempt is a big disaster, don't become discouraged. Part of developing routines is taking time to practice them and smooth out all the rough edges. Eventually, you'll develop the routine that works best for the needs of all family members in your home.

Developing a routine is worth all the work. By making adjustments in your life to create a routine, eventually your child will go to bed earlier, sleep longer, behave better, and you will be enjoying more recuperative time for yourself in the evenings as well.

"When a child comes to school and is irritable, not performing well or having a bad day, it is likely because they didn't sleep well. Some kids are kind of misunderstood in behavior problems because they are sleep-deprived. Whatever is keeping them up, they don't get enough rest, and you can see it the next day in their behavior. They are lethargic and not involved."

- Joe Cook

CONCLUSION

"Parenting is not a job, it's an adventure, so enjoy the journey..."

*C*hildren don't listen to your lectures, they model your example. As the parent, you are their number one role model. Even if you'd rather not be, this is an irrevocable honor (or nightmare) bestowed on all parents. It's a nightmare if you try to fight this responsibility, but if you've read this far, then parenting is sure to be the most wonderful journey of your life as you practice the methods in this book.

Relax and enjoy the journey. Parenting is a process, and it's a shame to miss out on soaking up the precious moments with your children. All too soon they will be grown-ups and away from home. Now is the prime time to enjoy their sweetness, innocence, purity, brilliance, and delight in the simple moments of joy and connection together.

When in doubt, just treat them how you would want to be treated and focus on establishing a strong sense of connection; you'll be over half way to overcoming any obstacle together. If you are courageous and zestful in your approach to the challenges of life, then so will your children be. Show them how wonderful life can be.

Please share your journey with us on Facebook! Come join the conversation, meet other happy-child parents, ask us questions, and let's all enjoy raising happy kids together! Go to: www. facebook.com/raisinghappykids

"Children learn to smile from their parents."

- Shinichi Suzuki

BONUSES

All of the following bonuses come with the book and are available for the purchaser of the book to access for free online. Simply email your book purchase receipt to support@parentlearningclub.com, and we'll send you the link where you can download them.

1 The 7-Week Effective Alternatives to Punishment

E-Coaching Course

You probably feel deep down that punishment is not always the best way to discipline your child. If you're like most parents, you probably find yourself punishing your child more often than you'd like. When your child is misbehaving and out of control, it's difficult to know what else to do.

You do have options, however, and we are going to share seven of them with you. These seven techniques work, and they are NOT based on punishment, rewards, or a bribing system! Instead, these seven ways of disciplining use a combination of "magic words" and "refocusing" techniques which dissolve arguments instantly.

Shouting as a form of discipline models the wrong behavior and it can end up leaving your child confused, fearful, and full of distrust. In this course, you will learn techniques for effectively communicating with your child and creating an atmosphere of respect.

This e-course will teach you to first evaluate the behavior and get to the root of the problem. Once you understand why your child is behaving in such a way, you can implement techniques to solve the problem.

You'll get this popular e-course FREE, delivered conveniently to your email inbox over a seven-week period.

Why by email, and why spread over seven weeks? We've found this is the best way to learn. It's convenient, easy, and you won't forget about it. Learning all seven techniques at once is overwhelming, and people only remember one or two that way.

Each week you will receive a new "Alternative to Punishment." You can use the technique for one whole week before starting the next one. By the end of the seven weeks, you will have a new repertoire of tactics to improve your child's behavior!

11 Common Super Foods That Super-Charge Your Child's Brain

Easy-to-Follow Diet Tips to Help with Child Misbehavior, ADD, ADHD, Obesity, and Poor Health
Downloadable and Printable E-Book

It is no secret that diet has a profound effect on mood, stress levels, energy, and overall health. A poor diet not only leads to obesity, it can affect behavior, especially in children. Choosing the right foods for your children can increase their ability to concentrate, give them more energy, and protect them from bacteria and viruses.

This is a compilation of eleven powerful foods that support brain function while simultaneously improving whole body health and strengthening the immune system. Including these eleven super foods in your family's diet will provide your children with particular vitamins, minerals, and fatty acids they need for proper mental development.

Want to know exactly what makes an apple so healthy? We've broken down these super foods and identified the exact ingredients that do the body such good.

Many of these foods are familiar, while others are less common. But you'll be glad to know that all of them are foods kids love! They are simple and easy to include in everyday meals.

If your child's behavior has become a challenge and interferes with success in school or relationships in the home, diet could be the culprit. This e-book includes tips for replacing unhealthy foods with the eleven super foods and ultimately solving behavior issues.

This is especially helpful for children diagnosed with ADD and ADHD.

You get this $19.95 e-book for FREE!

3 The Parenting Guide Super-Pack

Teaching Children Respect, Post-Natal Depression, 5 Reasons to Stop Saying "Good Job," Teaching Through Love Instead of Fear, and MORE
Six Downloadable and Printable Reports

With this bonus, you will actually get SIX items wrapped up into one!

Contained in this material are the answers to many of your parenting questions, provided by world-famous parenting experts including Pam Leo, Alfie Kohn, and others. These authors have generously allowed us to offer you these unique e-books for a limited time.

How often do you hear, "Kids these days have no respect"? If a child lacks respect, chances are they never learned it. The way you speak greatly affects your children, and these e-books will guide you on how to communicate with your child in a way that models respect. Furthermore, you will learn ways of disciplining that don't cause a child to feel ashamed, belittled, or ridiculed.

These e-books will give parents powerful tools for modeling behavior that will teach love instead of hate, thus diminishing the problem of bullying that has become prevalent in schools.

Learn to teach your children conflict resolution by practicing it in your own daily life.

Help your children navigate this complicated world. These e-books are a must-read for all parents who have children growing up in our modern society.

Valued at over $9.99 each, you are getting an enormous value for FREE!

4

How to Raise a Happy and Cooperative Child with Half the Effort

An exclusive interview with Naomi Aldort, PhD
Audio MP3 – Three hours

Ever wish you could teach your children to behave without using punishment? If you're like most parents, you may rely on it to teach your children rules. In this exclusive, never-before-heard interview, parenting expert and author Naomi Aldort clears up the misconception that punishment is the only effective way to raise cooperative children. She explains how to create an environment that naturally sets limits instead of imposing them.

Aldort also identifies the ingredients that go into raising a happy, secure child. Children develop a strong sense of self when they know they are cared for, that they can express themselves, and that they are being heard. They will trust their parents and will behave well because they want to, not because they want to please the parent.

In this interview, Ashley Ryan asks the burning questions on the minds of all parents. It contains ideas and solutions to challenges that all mothers and fathers face today. You'll discover practical information and many techniques you can put into practice right now! And it comes in a convenient audio MP3 format, so you can listen to it anytime.

This three-hour set is an exclusive bonus when you buy *Democratic Parenting!* And it's yours FREE.

What Every Parent Needs to Know about Discipline, Punishment, and Rules

An exclusive interview with Dr. Peter Haiman
Audio MP3 – One hour

Don't miss the valuable knowledge contained in this exclusive interview with Dr. Peter Haiman, a nationally recognized educational psychologist and expert on child and adolescent rearing. He will explain the basics of his Diagnostic Child Rearing approach designed to develop value-based children. His method is a simple, three-step process.

Parents, teachers, or anyone who deals with adolescents will learn from Dr. Haiman's extensive research. Children misbehave for a reason, and Dr. Haiman will teach you how to uncover the underlying cause so that you can treat the root of the frustration. Once you know the cause, then you can work on meeting the needs of the child. He also outlines the importance of looking at ourselves and how we were raised as well as the way society affects our children.

Dr. Haiman asserts that if we are fully meeting our children's needs, there will be no need for punishment, which only adds to the frustration and causes the misbehavior. He also addresses the misconception that meeting our children's needs will spoil them.

Also in this interview, Dr. Haiman models the language you can use to effectively praise your children and how to encourage them to express their feelings.

Learn the *dos* and *don'ts* of raising emotionally healthy, responsible children by following Dr. Haiman's approach. This interview is full of incredibly useful tips to help make disciplining your child much less stressful and much more successful.

We've had more than one parent tell us that what they learned from this interview alone was worth every penny of the book—and they loved the book too!

For a limited time, this one-hour audio recording is yours free when you buy *Democratic Parenting*!

6 How to Raise a Resilient Child

With exclusive interview with Dr. Robert Brooks
Audio MP3 – Three hours

In this compelling interview, Dr. Robert Brooks reveals the four words that cause children to be more cooperative. He also divulges the secrets of child communication and how you can have more respectful and empathetic interactions with your child from the moment of birth.

Based on extensive research in the area of resilience, Dr. Brooks explains how to raise a child with a "resilient mindset" who can successfully deal with stress and pressure, bounce back from adversity, and have an optimistic outlook on life.

Dr. Brooks holds a doctorate of clinical psychology from Clark University and is on the faculty of Harvard Medical School. He is a parenting expert and an internationally acclaimed author of numerous books including *Raising Resilient Children* and *Raising a Self-Disciplined Child*.

Dr. Brooks also offers parents valuable information on discipline and how to teach children that their behavior is their choice. He encourages parents to empower their children with tools for problem solving and learning from their mistakes.

This amazing interview digs deep for invaluable information and tactics for really getting through to your child. Listening to this recording offers the unique chance to open the door to better communication, and it's yours free when you order the *Democratic Parenting*!

ACKNOWLEDGMENTS

I would like to thank the following people whose support, inspiration, contribution and work was involved in the creation of this book.

First, I would like to thank Ashley Olivia Ryan, who originally wrote a book called *From Misbehaviour to Great Behavior* and was a contributing author in *The Happy Child Guide* series, both of which were the original inspirations for *Democratic Parenting*. Ashley continues to offer courses on ParentLearningClub.com for parents to learn how to apply these principles in their lives. Without Ashley's encouragement and initial spark, this book would not be here today.

To my parents, who loved and raised me wholesomely and were the first ones who taught me about parenting. May you live to play with your great, great, grandchildren!

To my ultimate parenting guru and the reason for this book; my son. Also to my nieces, nephews and all the children whom I am blessed to meet. You are the living angels of the earth who keep us adults on track despite ourselves. Our children show us the true definition of "unconditional love."

My sincere appreciation goes out to Isaac Romano, who started as a stranger in a coffee shop and soon changed my life, my family's life, and now every life who is transformed by this work. Isaac was the first person to introduce me to democratic parenting and I had the good fortune of working closely with him over many years. He was also the contributing editor on the 4th edition of *The Happy Child Guide*.

My appreciation goes out to Aletha Solter, Patty Wipfler, Pam Leo, Alfie Kohn, Jean Liedloff, Bryan Post, Naomi Aldort, Aloka Marti, Anne Savage, Magda Gerber, Frederick Froebel, Rudolf Dreikurs, Rudolf Steiner, Maria Montessori and Alfred Adler, whose pioneering lives were dedicated to evolving child development. Many of their theories, principles and methods have been integrated into this work.

My deepest gratitude goes to Bruce Spurr - my good friend and our captain in the crow's nest who's raw enthusiasm and reservoir of grit has seen this project through to completion. Keeping the helm firmly heading towards the betterment of the world through more smiling children, Bruce is responsible for this book's existence. Big thanks to the whole ParentLearningClub.com team for keeping the ship in the water.

Finally, I wish to extend my heart out to all the parents who give *Democratic Parenting* a try. Without your support, this book would never have seen the light of day. Thank you all for your continued encouragement. May your path be lit by the sound of giggling children.

"How to really love a child, be there.
Say yes as often as you can.
Let them bang on pots and pans.
If they're crabby put them in water.
Read books out loud with joy.
Go find elephants and kiss them.
Encourage silly. Giggle a lot.
Remember how really small they are.
Search out the positive.
Keep the gleam in your eye.
Go see a movie in your pajamas.
Teach feelings.
Realize how important it is to be a child.
Plan to build a rocket ship.
Stop Yelling.
Invent pleasures together.
Surprise them.
Express your love. A lot.
Children are Miraculous."

— *SARK*

INDEX

BIBLIOGRAPHY

Aldort, N. (2011). *Raising Our Children, Raising Ourselves: Transforming parent-child relationships from reaction and struggle to freedom, power and joy.* Book Publisher network.

Anderson, C. A., & Bushman, B. J. (2001, September). Effects of Violent Video Games on Agressive Behavior, Agressive Cognition, Aggressive Affect, Physiological Arousal, and Prosocial Behavior: A Meta-Analytic Review of the Scientific Literature. *Psychological Science, 12*(5), 353-359.

Anonymous. (2006). *FDA Statement on European Asparthame Study.* U.S. Food and Drug Administration. Washington: U.S. Food and Drug Administration.

Anonymous. (2007, September). Leave No New Mexico Child Inside. *Building Brides to the outdoors.* Sierra Club.

Anonymous. (2009, 07 23). Study nails secret of child sleep. *BBC News.*

Anonymous. (n.d.). *Sheet 15 - Children and Violence in the Media.* Retrieved from Cuilding a Culture of Peace - - Kit: http://www.peace.ca/sheet15.htm

Armstrong, T. (1997). *The Myth of the A.D.D Child:50 Ways to Improve Your Child's Behavior and Attention Span Without Drugs, Labels, or Coercion.* Plume.

Association, A. P. (2004, February 19). Research in Action. *Research in Action.*

Bakley, N. (2004). *More Mudpies: 101 Alternatives to Television.* Tricycle Press.

Bateman, B., Warner, J. O., Hutchinson, E., Dean, T., Rowlandson, P., Gant, c., et al. (2004). Food and Behavior Research. *Disease in Childhood,* 506-511.

Baughman, F. A., & Hovey, C. (2006). *The ADHD Fraud: How psychiatry Makes 'Patients' of Normal Children.* Trafford Publishing.

Baumrind, D. (1971). Current patterns of parental authority. *Developmental Psychology, 4*(1), 1-103.

Baumrind, D. (1978). Rearing competent children. In W. Damon (Ed.), *Child Development today and tomorrow* (pp. 349-378). San Fransisco: Jossey-Bass.

Baumrind, D. (1991). The Influence of parenting style on adolescent competence ans substance use. *Journal of Early Adolescence, 11*(1), 56-95.

Bernard, G. (1990). Natural Justice: A pilot study in evaluating and responding to criminal behavior as as environment phenomenon. *International Journal of Biosocial Medical Research, 12*, pp. 41-68.

Block, M. A. (1997). *No More Ritalin: Treating Adhd Without Drugs.* Kensington.

Bock, S. J., Bock, K., & Bruning, N. P. (1999). *Natural Relief for Your Child's Asthma: A Guide to Controlling Symptoms & Reducing Your Child's Dependence on Drugs.* Harpercollins Trade Sales.

Brooks, R., & Goldstein, S. (2007). *Raising a Self-Disciplined Child: Help Your Child Become More Responsible, Confident, and Resilient.* McGraw-Hill.

Byford, J. (n.d.). *Children in Nature.* Retrieved from www.aci-net.org/bw/08fall/children_in_nature.ppt

Cave, S., & Mitchell, D. (2001). *What Your Doctor May Not Tell You About(TM) Children's Vaccinations.* Grand Central Publishing.

Christakis, D. A., DiGiuseppe, D. L., & Zimmerman, F. J. (2004, April 1). Early Television Exposure and Subsequent Attentional Problems in Children. *Pediatrics, 113*(4-A), pp. 708-713.

Coleman, B. C. (1997, August 15). Study : Do not Spank.

Colwell, J., & Payne, J. (2000, August). Negative Correlates of Computer Game Play in Adolescents. *British Journal of Psychology, 91*(3), 295-310.

Cook, D. E., Kestenbaum, C., Honaker, M. L., Ratcliff Anderson, E., American Academy of Family Phsicians, & American Psychiatric Association. (2000, July 26). Joint Statement on the Impact of Entertainment Violence on Children. United-States of America: Congressional Public Health Summit.

Coyne, S. M., & Whitehead, E. (2008, July 9). Indirect Aggression in Animated Disney Film. *Journal of Communication, 28*(2), 382-395.

Dengate, S., & A., R. (2002, August). Controlled trial of cumulative behavioural effects of a common bread preservative. *Journal of Pediatrics and Child Health, 38*(4), 373-376.

DesMaisons, K. (2004, July 27). Little Sugar Addicts: End the Mood Swings, Meltdowns, Tantrums, and Low Self-Esteem in Your Child Today. 288. Three Rivers Press.

Dreikus, R., & Soltz, V. (1991). *Children: The Challenge : The Classic Work on Improving Parent-Child Relations--Intelligent, Humane & Eminently Practical.* Plume.

Durant, R. H., Champion, H., & Wolfson, M. (2006, August 1). The Relationship Between Watching Professional Wrestling on Television and Engaging in Date Fighting Among High School Students. *Pediatrics, 118*(2), 265-272.

England, P., & Horowitz, R. (1998). *Birthing from Within: An Extra-Ordinary Guide to Childbirth Preparation.* Partera.

Flaws, B. (1999). *Keeping Your Child Healthy with Chinese Medecine: A Parent's guide to the Care and Prevention of Common Childhood Diseases.* Boulder, Colorado: Blue Poppy Press.

Foundation, T. H. (2006). *The Media Family: Electronic Media in the Lives of Infants, Toddlers, Preschoolers, and Their Parents.* The Henry J. Kaiser Family Foundation.

Frey II, W. H. (1985). *Crying: The Mystery of Tears.* Canada: HarperCollins.

Fyfe, K. (2006). *Wolves in Sheeps Clothing : A content Analysis of Children<s Television.* Parents television council.

Gaskin, I. M. (2003). *Ina May's Guide to Childbirth.* Bantam.

Gaskin, I. M. (2003). *Spiritual Midwifery.* New Millennium Edition.

Gerber, M., & Johnson, A. (1997). *Your Self-Confident Baby: How to Encourage Your Child's Natural Abilities -- From the Very Start.* Wiley.

Giraldi, N. L., Shaywitz, S. E., Shaywitz, B. A., Marchione, K., Fleischman, S. J., Jones, T. W., et al. (1995, October). Blunted catecholamine responses after glucose ingestion in children with attention deficit disorder. *Pediatric Research, 38*(4), 539-542.

Glasser, H. (2005). *101 Reasons to Avoid Ritalin Like the Plague: Including 1 Great Reason Why it's Almost Always Unnecessary.* Nutured Heart Publication.

Glasser, H., & Block, M. (2008). *All Children Flourishing - Igniting the Greatness of our Children.* Nurthured Hearts Publications.

Griffiths, M. (1999). Violent Video Games and Aggression: A Review of the Literature. *Aggression and Violent Behavior, 4*(2), 203-212.

Grossman, D., & DeGaetano, G. (1999). *Stop Teaching our Kids to Kill.* New York: Random House.

Group, S. A. (2009). *Keeping Children Healthy in California's Child Care Environments.* California Health and Human Service Agency, California Department of Education. Sacramento: California Department of Education.

Gruber, J. (1985). Physical Activity and Self-Esteem development in children: A meta-analysis. (G. A. Stull, & H. M. Eckert, Eds.) *Academy Papers, 19*, 30-48.

Gunter, B. (1994). The Question of Media Violence. In J. Bryant, & D. Zillman (Eds.), *Media Effects - Advances in Theory and Research* (pp. 162-211). Hillsdale, New Jersey: Lawrence Erlbaum Associates.

Hastings, B. (2001). Dopamine Oxidation Alters Mitochondrial Respiration and Induces Permeability Transition in Brain Mitochondria. *Journal of Neurochemistry, 73*(3), pp. 1127-1137.

Hillman, C. (n.d.). *The FITKIDS Afterschool Program.* University of Illinois, Neurocognitive Kinesiology Laboratory, Department of Kinesiology and Community Health.

Huesmann, R. L., Lagerspetz, K., & Leonard, E. D. (1984, September). Intervening variables in the TV violence-agression relation: Evidence from two countries. *Developmental Psychology, 20*(5), 746-775.

Ishikawa, S., & Raine, A. (2003, April 14). Obstetric Complications and Aggression. In r. Tremblay, R. Barr, & R. Peters (Eds.), *Encyclopedia of Childhood Development* (pp. 1-6). Montreal, Quebec, Canada: Centre of Excellence for Early Childhood Development.

Juneau, D. (2011, November 15). *School Programs: School Nutritional Programs.* Retrieved from Montana, Office of Public Instruction: http://opi.mt.gov/Programs/SchoolPrograms/School_Nutrition/

Kotti, T. J., Ramirez, D. M., Pfeiffer, B. E., Huber, K. M., & Russell, D. W. (2006, February 27). Brain cholesterol turnover required for geranylgeraniol production and learning in mice. *Proceedings of National Academcy of Sciences of the United States, 103*(10), 3869-3874.

Krugman, H. E. (1971, February). We act on print, but TV acts on us, according to G.E. Latest Study of Brain Wave Measures of Media Involvement. *Journal of Advertising Research, 11*(1), 3-9.

Landfield, P. W. (1990). *The role of glucocorticoids in brain aging and Alzheimer's disease: An integrative physiological hypothesis.* University of Kentucky College of Medicine, Department of Pharmacology. University of Kentucky Press.

Leo, P. (2005). *Connection Parenting: Parenting Through Connection Instead of Coercion, Through Love Instead of Fear.* Wyatt-Mackenzie Publishing.

Littlefield Cook, J., & Cook, G. (2008). *Child Development: Principles and Perspectives.* Allyn & Bacon.

Liu, J., Raine, A., Venables, P. H., & Mednick, S. A. (2004, November 1). Malnutrition at age 3 Years and Externalizing Behavior Problems at Ages 8, 11 and 17 Years. *The American Journal of Psychiatry, 161*(11), 2005-2013.

McMillian, H. L., Boyle, M. H., Wong, M. Y., Duku, E. K., Fleming, J. E., & Walsh, C. A. (1999, October 5). Slapping, spanking and psychiatric disorders. *Canadian Medical Association, 161*(7).

Miller, N. B., Cowan, P. A., Cowen, C. P., & Hetherington, E. M. (1993). Externalizing in preschoolers and early adolescents: a cross study replication of a family model. *Developmental Psychology, 29*(1), 3-18.

244

Mukherjee, N. (2009, September 22). *Signs and Prevention of Dehydration: A Guide to Drinking Water.* Retrieved from Nutrition@Suite101: http://nita-mukherjee.suite101.com/signs-and-prevention-of-dehydration-a151405

Nielsen, C. (2009). *How Teens Use Media: A Nielsen report on the myths and realities of teen medi trends.* The Nielsen Company.

O'Brian, S. (2007). *Food Additives Linked to Child Aggression.* Retrieved from information Liberation: http://www.informationliberation.com/?id=21399

Paavonen, J., Raikkonen, K., Lahti, J., Komsi, N., Heinonen, K., Pesonen, A.-K., et al. (2009, May 1). Short Sleep Duration and Behaviroal Symptoms of Attention-Deficit/Hperactivitiy Disorder in Healthly 7- to-8-Year Old Children. *Pediatrics, 123,* e857-e864.

Ransford, C. P. (1982). A Role for Amines in the Antidepressant Effect of Excercise: a review. *Medicine and Science in Sports and Excerise, 14*(1), 1-10.

Reid, K. (2002). Sleep-Deprivation Among Teenagers ay Impact Academic and Behavioral Performance. *54th Annual Meeting of the American Academy of Neurology.* Denver.

Richardson, A. J. (2005, May 1). The Oxford-Durham Study: A Randomized, Controlled Trial of Dietary Supplementation With Fatty Acids in Children With Developmental Coordination Disorder. *Pediatrics, 115*(5), 1360-1366.

Richardson, D. (n.d.). Guiding Young Children Series: Why Children Misbehave. *Oklahoma Cooperative Extension Service, 2325,* 1-8.

Rosenthal, r. (1986). Media Violence, Antisocial Behavior, and the Social Consequences of Small Effects. *Journal of Social Issues, 42*(3), 141-154.

Schmidt, M. E., Pempek, T. A., Kirkorian, H. L., Frankenfield Lund, A., & Anderson, D. R. (n.d.). The Effects of Background Television on the Toy Play Behavior of Very Young Children. *Society for Research in Child Development,* 1-40.

Selman, J. E. (2005, April 14). Attention Deficit-Hyperactivity Disorder - Correspondence. *New England Journal of Medicine, 352,* 1607-1608.

Sergueef, N. (2007). *Cranial Osteopathy for Infants, Children and Adolescents: A Practical Handbook.* A Churchill Livingstone Title.

Sigman, A. (2007). *Remotely Controlled.* London: Ebury / Random House.

Sigman, A. (2007, February). Visual Voodoo: the biological impact of watching TV. *Biologist, 54*(1), pp. 12-17.

Singer, D., & Singer, J. L. (2001). *Handbook of children and the media.* Thousand Oaks, CA: Sage Publishing Co.

Smits, J. A., Berry, A. C., Rosenfield, D., Powers, M. B., Behar, E., & Otto, M. W. (2008). Reducing Anxiety Sensitivity with Exercise. *Depress Anxiety, 25*(8), 689-699.

Soffritti, M., Belpoggi, F., Espoti, D. D., & Lambertini, L. (2005). Asparthame induces lymphomas and leukemias in rats. *European Journal of Oncology, 10*(2), 107-116.

Solter, A. J. (1989). *Helping Your Children Flourish*. Shining Star Press.

Solter, A. J. (1997). *Tears and Tantrums: What to Do When Babies and Children Cry*. Shining Star Press.

Solter, A. J. (2001). *The Aware Baby*. Shining Star Press.

Steiner, R., & Sagarin, S. K. (2003). *What Is Waldorf Education?: Three Lectures*. Steiner Books.

Steiner, R., Everett, R., & Sloan, D. (1996). *The Child's Changing Consciousness (Foundations of Waldorf Education)*. Anthroposophic Press.

Tamborini, R., Chory, R. M., Lachlan, K., Westerman, D., & Skalski, P. (2008, July-September). Talking Smack: Verbal Aggression. *Communication Studies, 59*(3), 242-258.

Taylor, F. A., Kuo, F. E., & Sullivan, W. C. (2001). Coping with ADD: The surprising connection to green play settings. *Environmental Behavior, 33*(1), 54-77.

Tenpenny, S. J. (2008). *Saying No to Vaccines: A Resource Guide for All Ages*. Cleveland, Ohio: NMA Media Press.

Thompson Gershoff, E. (2002). Corporal Punishments by Parents and Associated Child Behaviors and Experience: A Meta-Analytic and Theoretical Review. *Psychological Bulletin, 128*(4), pp. 539-579.

Weiss, L. H., & Schwarz, J. C. (1996). The relationship between parenting types and older adolescents, personality, academic achievement, adjustment and substance use. *Child Development, 67*(5), 2101-2114.

Wipfler, P. (1990). *Listening to Children: Healing Children's Fears*. Parents Leadership Institute.

Wipfler, P. (1995). *Setting Limits with Children*. Parents Leadership Institute.

Wirth, F. (2001). *Prenatal Parenting: The Complete Psychological and Spiritual Guid to Loving Your Unborn Child*. New York: Harpercollins Trade Sales Deptarment.

Zaalberg, A., Nijman, H., Bulten, E., Stroosma, L., & Van der Staak, C. (2010, March/April). Effects of nutritional supplements on aggression, rule-breaking, and psychopathology among young adult prisoners. *Agressive Behavior, 36*(2), pp. 117-126.

Zand, J., Rountree, R., & Walton, R. (2003). *Smart Medicine for a Healthier Child*. New York: Avery.

246